W9-CKH-302

Made in Heaven, Settled in Court

Made in Heaven, Settled in Court

by Marvin M. Mitchelson

PUBLISHED BY J.P. TARCHER, INC., LOS ANGELES

Distributed by Hawthorn Books, Inc., New York

Dedication

To all my wives—and husbands, too.

Copyright © 1976 by Marvin Mitchelson
All rights reserved

Library of Congress Catalog Card Number: 74-27652

ISBN: 0-87477-037-8

Manufactured in the United States of America

Published by J.P. Tarcher, Inc.
9110 Sunset Blvd., Los Angeles, Calif. 90069

Published simultaneously in Canada by
Prentice-Hall of Canada, Ltd.
1870 Birchmount Rd., Scarborough, Ontario

1 2 3 4 5 6 7 8 9 0

Contents

Preface

Incidents and observations in the following pages are taken from divorce cases I have been privileged to handle during my twenty years in the practice of law. Many of the incidents were widely publicized during the heat of courtroom battles. I have revealed no confidences and, I hope, evoked no unpleasant memories which have not been made less painful by the passage of time.

By telling each incident and story as faithfully as memory, case files, and courtroom transcripts can insure, I have tried to show, from the inside, what it's like to go through one of the most personally devastating experiences one can face. In doing so, I have tried to choose those cases which best illustrate important points of law or significant aspects of human behavior under marital stress.

Use of real names and real people is in no way intended to titillate public curiosity or convince the reader my life in court is any more impressive and important than that of any other lawyer. All of us frequently lead clients who are publicly nameless through divorce proceedings with far less dramatic problems than those outlined here. The pain, pathos, and sometimes gallows humor which hovers over marital disintegration is as real and personal to the ordinary person as it is to the wealthy and famous.

I hope my experiences may provide some measure of comfort to the many persons involved in divorce who need reassurances that the terrible dilemmas before them have been faced and surmounted by others.

Marvin M. Mitchelson
August 1976

CHAPTER ONE

The Third Party

It has often been said that "marriages are made in heaven." In attempting to "set asunder" that which God has joined together and man has infinitely complicated, the divorce lawyer is required to be many things. Playing the roles of sage conciliator, fierce protector, fellow dreamer, hard-nosed realist, part-time psychiatrist, confessor, accountant, referee, and detective is all supposed to be part of the ideal divorce lawyers' repertoire. That is precisely why the "ideal" divorce lawyer cannot be found either in heaven or on earth, for that person simply doesn't exist.

During my twenty years of practice primarily as a divorce attorney, at one time or another I've been called upon to play all of these roles, with varying degrees of success—and failure, particularly when trying to play them all at once. Yet, a client's loneliness, coupled with the burdens of bitterness, guilt, frustration, and fear, often force me and my colleagues to attempt the impossible.

Recognizing the need for that attempt is perhaps the most important thing I've learned since guiding my first distraught client through the not-so-velvet jungle of divorce court many wives, husbands, and years ago.

Divorce proceedings are often as emotion-charged as murder trials. Long suppressed anger, hurt, and resentment may pour out, along with a sense of outraged betrayal. Ego is matched against ego, with vanity or self-justification often the prime emotion. Divorce is positive proof of failure. Each party is secretly determined to emerge blameless, or at least be reassured that, under the circumstances, they could have acted no differently.

Into this charged atmosphere, the divorce lawyer comes as a third party in what is an inherently two-party relationship. Clients often view the lawyer as a hired gun whose main task is to outshoot the opposing hired guns and bring the ex-spouse to his or her knees. But sometimes, if the lawyer proves too good a champion, he can end up being branded the villain by his own client.

Something like this happened with one of my first major divorce clients. She was a woman who had an almost morbid distrust of lawyers, and warned me repeatedly she would never accept a penny less than $1 million in settlement. When I finally brought her an offer exceeding that amount, she turned on me completely outraged: "You can't do this to the father of my children! You can't just pauperize him this way!"

Such outbursts are a part of the client's ever-changing emotional pattern that turns a divorce lawyer into a chameleon with a law book. With inconsistency about the only consistent factor in a divorce client's makeup, divorce lawyers frequently find themselves in the uncomfortable position of facing adversaries on both sides of the counsel table, with the other attorney often the less formidable opponent.

Until recently, there was also another bitter ingredient for the emotional stew of most divorce proceedings: divorce laws with the concept of guilt or fault. Today, many states are removing this concept from their statutes. California now dissolves marriages with the simple statement by either party that "irreconcilable differences have led to an irremediable breakdown of the marriage." Not even a corroborating witness is necessary under this "no-fault" concept.

Under the old law, a number of specific grounds were permitted, ranging from infidelity to mental cruelty, and judges could award a greater portion to the "innocent" spouse, the one considered the least responsible for the marriage's failure.

The old way resulted in a lot of embarrassing accusations about who slept with whom, and revealed a number of socially undesirable personal habits in certain public figures. But the average person still felt he or she could get *justice* only if the other spouse's social or moral perfidy was exposed in open court, and this aspect sometimes encouraged couples to blacken each other's names solely to gain revenge or greater financial reward. However, in cases where the conduct of one party was particularly odious, lawyers often had a better chance to work an out-of-court settlement. I often found the possibility of having one's dirty linen washed in public created a state of mind conducive to reaching a reasonable settlement without undergoing the ordeal of a trial.

Taking away the forum for making a public spectacle of people's private lives was, of course, one of the primary purposes of no-fault divorce, along with the idea that if the name-calling and accusations were eliminated, it would remove much of the antagonistic aftermath. However, in many cases the acrimony and vicious in-fighting still go on. This is particularly true in custody matters, where children are the main pawns, often being bartered for revenge and cash.

Another notable change since the new law went into effect seems to be a less avid public interest in divorce trials. The focus of the wrangling isn't behavior as much as it is property. In California, for example, husbands, realizing the no-fault concept rewards a bad spouse in equal measure as it would a good one, conceal assets with increasing frequency and cleverness. Since husbands have traditionally controlled family finances, the new system forces a divorce lawyer representing women to hire or become financial expert and sleuth more than ever before.

I once discovered a completely fictitious Mexican branch company had been created and maintained over a long period of time by the husband of a woman I represented. The losses attributed to this nonexistent firm by the husband (who had had previous experience with divorce property settlements) would have given him a community property-exempt nest egg in six figures. In another case, my client's husband pursuaded her to sign away rights to more than $13 million worth of stock in the mistaken belief it was a mere formality to create a trust fund for their children.

When it comes to property rights, women are likely to be at a disadvantage regardless of the divorce laws in any state. The disadvantages are multiplied when people begin married life with very little fortune and end it at a time when considerable wealth has accumulated. The wife of a man who fights his way to the upper levels of the corporate jungle seldom has any idea of how much he's made, since reliance on her husband to make and invest money is one of the most traditional aspects of marriage. As the years go by, a conventional wife devotes herself to home and children, and has only vague ideas about the mortgage payments, interest rates, and taxes. When the personal world of a middle-aged housewife and mother is turned upside down by divorce, such a woman is apt to lack the hard business sense necessary to manage her own affairs, and financial panic is only the beginning of her many problems.

It is also an incontrovertible fact that a woman in today's youth-oriented culture is considered "old" at the same age a man reaches "the prime of life." That factor probably contributes more to the ultimate failure of marriage than anything else, and in the face of current social commitment to "sexual equality," it can turn a woman's already traumatic divorce experience into personal disaster.

As an added burden to her, the courts are beginning to think in terms of reducing spousal support, or alimony, both by limiting the amount and the length of payment. This trend may have little effect for young and childless women after relatively short marriages, but for the older woman who became housewife and mother at an early age and who has no marketable work skills, the problems of reentering the job market can be insurmountable.

This problem is particularly true in the field of entertainment, which has been the industry in which many of my own clients have been employed. Yesterday's star may be as forgotten as yesterday's headlines. Young actresses, particularly, who drop out for even a few years to be housewives often lose their chances for all time. By the time they come to a lawyer's office, many such women are so defeated that their self-esteem, and sometimes even their very sense of identity, has completely vanished.

Under the emotional stress of the sometimes drawn-out divorce proceedings, client and attorney can develop a close personal relationship. At this shattering time in their lives, clients need a friend and advisor to guide them through the trauma and to help them make the transition into a new lifestyle afterwards. When an attorney takes the time and effort to fill this need, it can help in every aspect of the case. If a client trusts the attorney as a friend, the lawyer's advice is more likely to be followed. As a result, the client is more apt to remain composed during emotion-charged periods of negotiation or trial, which leaves the lawyer free to concentrate on the opposing side, the issues at hand, and ways of resolving the conflict in question.

This personal involvement can occasionally elicit curious demands. Shortly after working out a shaky temporary agreement between a fiery-tempered actress and her equally hot-tempered producer husband, I was jarred out of my sleep by the bedside telephone.

"You can't let him get away with this!" the flame-haired actress shrieked, without one introductory comment. "He's disconnected it and taken it away!"

"Wait a minute," I mumbled. "Who did what disconnect?"

"My bidet!" she shouted. "I just came back from a party, and it's gone. . . . I went to the bathroom and there's nothing but empty space and pipes."

"Well, look," I said, still not fully awake, "you can always get a new one. With the kind of settlement you're going to get, you can buy half the bidets in France."

"I don't want half the bidets in France," she continued. "I want *my* bidet. What the hell kind of lawyer are you, anyway, letting him get away with something like this?"

A sleepy lawyer with an irritated bed partner, I thought to myself, as my Italian-born wife, Marcella, began her own lament about interrupted sleep, the lateness of the hour, and the "office hours" of some divorce lawyers.

"Look, it's three o'clock in the morning," I argued, in an attempt at rationality. "Let's talk about it tomorrow."

"Oh, no, we won't," she raged. "We'll talk about it right now! I want that bidet back even if we have to drag him off of it. So what are you going to do?"

Deciding that the only way to quiet her down was to placate her with plans, strategy, and proposed performance, I said, "Look, I'll get a *subpoena duces tecum,* or a *writ of habeus corpus* for it in the morning, and we'll also cite him into court for contempt."

After a minute of uncertain silence, she said, "You'll do all that?"

"First thing tomorrow," I promised, and hung up the phone. By now, my wife was sitting up in bed with a puzzled look on her face.

"Just what kind of talk was that?" she asked.

"Legal nonsense," I shrugged. "But it will get all three of us back to sleep."

It took a day and a half to get the bidet returned, which probably made it the most expensive bidet in or out of France, but it showed me the confusing, unrestrained emotions generated by separation and divorce of two personalities once so intimately joined. It showed the extent to which one party will go to spite the other, the no-limits-and-no-expense-spared crusade of the other to repossess an object that could easily be replaced, the strong need for a sense of justice in even so minor a matter, let alone the need to judiciously handle the larger issues of custody, child support, and property division.

At times like these, the personal approach to client relations might seem to get out of hand, but I don't think I'd want it any other way. The knowledge someone is still interested in them, and considers them of genuine value and worth, enables clients going through divorce to overcome their sense of isolation and restores their self-esteem. And the closeness that sometimes develops between lawyer and client can bring a sense of fulfillment that makes the practice of divorce law uniquely challenging and more exciting than any other profession in which I'd want to spend my time.

CHAPTER TWO

The Making of a Lawyer

Growing up in Los Angeles, like many young people during the Great Depression who read about the glittering life of Hollywood celebrities, I often dreamed about becoming a great actor. But as the only son of hard-working parents—my father was a building contractor, my mother a devoted homemaker—who had emigrated from Europe, I knew I was expected to enter a solid profession, one that was both respectable and responsible.

As the youngest of three children I felt that my mother expected a great deal of me throughout my childhood while she fearfully predicted the worst. When I enlisted in the Navy in 1946 soon after graduating from high school, where my only accomplishment had been to be the lightest man on the varsity football team, it only increased her oft-stated warning that I'd probably never amount to much. Boys who enlisted in the Navy were not, according to her, taking life seriously. Her convictions were reinforced when I launched into my Navy career with a typical rookie error. I wanted to learn how to use semaphore flags, so the first thing I did was step into a line of people volunteering to be trained as corpsmen. Unfortunately, the line was for medical corpsmen, not signal corpsmen, and I spent the next year as an operating room assistant on the cruiser U.S.S. *Columbus* sailing in Shanghai and mainland China waters.

That training, however, did kindle an interest in medicine, and my family was delighted when I wrote home to say I wanted to become a doctor—a proper profession at last. Things looked even better when I started playing football in intrafleet athletics, for I played just well enough to qualify after my discharge for a football scholarship at the University of Oregon in Eugene.

Word of the scholarship came through just before my father died, and I never had a chance to tell him. But his death turned me away from medicine as a career. For a long time I blamed the doctors for letting him die by not showing up at the hospital that Sunday morning in time to save him, and I wanted no part of the profession. I went ahead with the football scholarship, though, and entered the university in January of 1948.

Both of my sisters were married (in a double wedding cere-mony) while I was away at school, and when I came home for the summer my mother was alone, managing six apartment buildings all by herself. I decided right then not to go back to Oregon, but to stay and help her. After enrolling at Occidental College in Los Angeles, I went out for football, but broke my wrist on the first day of practice. It put a quick end to my football career and left me feeling thwarted at everything I wanted to do.

The next year, I transferred to UCLA, majoring in history. It was at some point in the next two years that I decided to study law. It was just a matter of elimination. After all, with medicine no longer of interest and having no inclination for teaching, law seemed to be all that was left if I were going to pursue a traditional profession.

My sisters, Marion and May, who had inherited my mother's critical abilities, agreed. What could be a better occupation, they said, for a person who was so argumentative, so fond of making speeches, so eager to grab center stage, and so prone to confuse wishful thinking with facts? Having read my share of Perry Mason stories, I had romanticized the law considerably. Just as I had once imagined myself a star of stage, operating room, and athletic field, I now visualized myself in a courtroom packed with spectators waiting breathlessly for me to persuade the jury to acquit my innocent client, while simultaneously exposing the real perpetrator of the crime.

After graduating from UCLA in 1953, I entered Southwestern University School of Law, a "workingman's" law school in downtown Los Angeles, and set out to find employment that would both bring in money and be useful in my intended career. One day I talked with a man who was a process server, and after he explained his work I knew I'd found the right kind of job.

A process server is a civil lawyer's messenger. Legally, a person doesn't become subject to the court's jurisdiction until he is informed of the action filed against him and the time his appearance is required. In civil litigation, where individuals are suing other individuals, lawyers must arrange to have all necessary legal papers served in their client's behalf, and it's the process server or a marshal who delivers the documents for them.

The pay for being a high-class delivery boy was good—if you knew how to work the system. The standard fee at that time was a dollar per document, plus thirty-five cents a mile for each separate service, measured from Los Angeles City Hall. (To this day, I know the distances from point to point in Los Angeles better than do most cab drivers.) Sometimes there was special compensation for difficult-to-serve persons, such as movie stars and other well-known people, who tended to be both hard to reach and reluctant to accept papers. Although rivalry for business between the process-serving organizations was keen, I managed, without letting them know it, to work for all three of the major L.A. process-serving firms at the same time. By carefully organizing my daily work load, I could often gather a dozen or more papers to be served in the same area and collect the mileage fees for each one. There were some months when I made more than $2,000, but I felt I earned it. While most people accepted papers with only a sullen comment or muttered insult or half-hearted effort to avoid service, there were a few who got physically abusive.

When the process server knocks, the door does not always open, and for those people who refused to see me, I had a standard ploy: I would simply open the complaint and start reading it at the top of my voice. As I started to yell out the details of purported frauds, business misconduct, or marital indiscretions, passersby would stop to listen and neighbors' windows would fly open. In seconds the door would be flung open and the paper snatched from my hands with accompanying curses.

Sometimes I was physically attacked. On two occasions angry women ripped first the coat and then the shirt off my back, and one went a number of steps further. I once had to serve a document involving a divorce action on a woman who lived in Sunland, a hillside community thirty miles from Los Angeles. Since I also had made a date to go to the movies that evening, I took the girl with me on the ride to Sunland. After finding the address I parked and, leaving my date in the car, walked up to the house which was set back from the road behind a picket fence with a little wooden gate. By the time I reached the porch, the woman was waiting for me. I identified myself and thrust out the paper. She made no move to accept it. "I'm getting sick and tired of being served all these goddamned papers," she muttered. "In fact, I'm getting so sick of it, I'm gonna shoot the next son of a bitch who comes up here with any!"

I should have dropped the paper and run. Contrary to popular belief, it isn't necessary to actually hand a person a paper. The service would still have been legal. But, instead, to save face in front of my date, I tried to placate the woman. I proffered the document again and said, "Well, in that case, I promise I won't serve you with any *more* papers."

At that, she snatched the document, and the next thing I knew I was looking into the barrel of a large pistol. "To hell with it. I'm not gonna wait for the next person," she said angrily. "I'm gonna shoot *you!* Now!"

I started backing away. "Look, lady," I stammered, "this is just a job to me. I'm doing it to put myself through school and pay my mother's medical bills. I don't mean anything personal. I'll take the paper back, if that's what you want." At that, I actually reached forward and took the paper out of her hand. I backed down the steps, apologizing all the way, and walked backward toward the gate. The gun didn't waver. Then, just as I turned to open the gate, she fired, and a bullet whistled past my left ear. I hurtled the hedge, sprinted for the car at a speed which would have qualified me for the Indianapolis 500, and drove as fast as I could to the closest phone booth to call the police.

Later I accompanied a patrol car back to the woman's house. This time when she answered the door—with gun in hand—the police quickly disarmed her. Before they led her away I again gave her the paper.

My fee for completing the service came to $10—all profit, since my date and I, figuring we had seen enough action for one night, never made it to the movies.

Most of my experiences, even with difficult subjects, were much less dramatic, and usually it was my imagination that was tested more than my courage. I used the standard ploys for people who tried to dodge service, such as pretending to deliver a package that had to be signed for personally. I developed a few touches of my own, too. At Christmas time, for instance, I wrapped documents up in tissue paper and red ribbon and passed them out like presents. I developed a reputation for being able to serve people nobody else could reach, especially entertainment figures, who seemed to be sued or were suing somebody most of the time. A few of them really put a strain on my resourcefulness.

One was British actress Joan Collins, who had decided she just wasn't going to be served in a particular domestic relations action. After several futile attempts to effect the service discreetly at her home, I realized it would have to be done in public or at the studio. Since most stars in Miss Collins's era traveled by closed limousine and were constantly surrounded by public relations men and studio aides, approaching her in public was next to impossible. Serving her at the studio didn't seem promising, either. The trade papers said she was engaged in a remake of *The Women* at MGM, and that studio had its own police force and was known as the toughest lot in Hollywood to crash.

However, I decided that one workman looked much like another to a studio guard and so early one morning I went over the fence dressed in the coveralls of a grip. After mingling with other workers for a while, I started picking up anything movable I could find. I'd carry it a few feet, put it down, and look for something else, all the while inching toward the sound stage where Miss

Collins was shooting. On the set I joined some stagehands who were putting up a wall and watched Miss Collins run through her next scene.

For my purposes the circumstances were ideal. The set was rigged as a library, and Miss Collins was supposed to enter from the rear and walk toward a door until the camera moved in for a close-up. I was standing less than three feet from the door. I realized, however, there were too many people around and I might not be able to serve the paper during the rehearsal, so I waited. Finally, there was the call, "Lights. Camera. Action!" The red light flashed, work ceased, cameras began to turn.

Miss Collins started toward the doorway. As she raised her head to speak her lines, I moved in, spoke *my* line, thrust the papers at her—and ran like hell. On the stage behind me there was pandemonium. I raced for the studio wall and leaped over it at a spot I had prepared for my emergency exit.

Later, when the picture was released, I went to see it. I wasn't in it, of course. My big scene ended up on the cutting room floor.

Once I managed to serve a superstar in public. Sophia Loren had been as inaccessible as Joan Collins, but I caught her after a Directors' Guild premiere of a new picture. She came out of the theater surrounded by autograph seekers, and I immediately knew I'd never be able to force my way close enough before she reached her car. So, pretending to be a theater guard, I started pushing people out of the way, shouting, "Come on, now! Let's move back, people! Give Miss Loren room to get to her car, please!" People began getting out of the way. I made it to the limousine and smilingly opened the door for her. When she turned to thank me, I delivered my little message and the papers and backed away amidst a torrent of angry Italian words which lost nothing in the translation.

Perhaps my most memorable escapade in process serving, how-ever, involved Louis B. Mayer, the legendary movie giant who had built a virtually impenetrable barrier around himself. I tried for a long time to get to him at home and at the studio to serve him with papers involving a large lawsuit against his studio, but he just couldn't be reached. Then I read in the trade papers, an ever useful source of information, that he was going to be honored at a dinner for his great contributions to the industry over the years.

I put on a tuxedo and arrived at the hotel early to survey the security measures. I watched as people entered the big dining room, had their invitations checked, and then were escorted to the proper table. Seeing there was no way for me to pass as a guest, I walked briskly through the entryway, flipped open my wallet, and mumbled, "Hotel staff." As it so often does, the obvious gambit worked.

While Mayer received his awards, I stood quietly in the wings, my papers wrapped in a scroll and tied with a ribbon. Finally, there was a lull in the proceedings. I stepped forward and he turned toward me, smiling broadly. I extended my offering and, speaking softly, told him what it was. For an instant, his eyes flashed with the kind of outrage the powerful can show when their private worlds have been invaded. Then he chuckled, slipped the papers in his pocket, and muttered, "Good work, son. Now, beat it!"

I served my last paper, involving a rather minor breach-of-contract suit, on actress Polly Bergen. It was just after I'd passed the bar examination, and so with a light heart I went to serve Miss Bergen at her Beverly Hills Hotel suite.

I knocked on the door, and her husband answered. When I explained my presence, he turned angry. "Polly's got no time for this!" he yelled. "Get outta here!"

"Look," I said, "it's only a minor thing she'll have to accept eventually anyway. Why not make it easy for everybody?"

"I said get out!" he shouted. "Get lost! She's busy!"

The noise brought Miss Bergen into the front room. I quickly told her what the document's contents were, flipped it to her over her husband's shoulder, and turned to walk away. But I hadn't taken ten steps before he was on my back.

Perhaps it was the knowledge that I was at last officially an attorney, or maybe it was simply the accumulation of those years of abuse, but something inside me snapped, and instead of running I returned the punch he threw at me. After we traded several blows some hotel employees finally separated us, and an assistant manager loudly warned me that if I ever came back to the hotel he'd call the police—a threat never carried out in the many times I've been back since.

Being a process server was important experience, and did a lot more for me than just finance law school. It taught me a great deal about court processes, especially the strategic advantage in the proper use of subpoenas, and gave me some understanding of lawsuits and how much emotion they can engender. It also allowed me to meet many people who have been helpful to me through the years. And if nothing else, it has enabled me to tell my own process servers since then how to get maximum results.

After I passed the bar in 1957, I decided that before making the rounds of the big law firms in search of employment and a chance for an eventual junior partnership, I should first try going it alone. I therefore rented a small office in Beverly Hills and sent out announcements. I also threw a party, but most of the friends who came already had lawyers, were lawyers, or had no need for lawyers. My first clients, then, came to me literally off the street and in unexpected ways.

Actually, I had my very first client before I even had my license—that is, after I passed the bar exam, but before I was sworn in. One of the cocktail waitresses at the old Melody Room nightclub-restaurant, which I occasionally frequented on Hollywood's Sunset Strip, asked me to defend her against a bad check charge. In fact, she offered me one hundred dollars for a retainer—and wrote me a check. As tactfully as possible, I asked if she could give me cash instead. She did so (by cashing a check at the drugstore next door), and I rushed home to show my mother my first fee. Dealing with apartment tenants had made her sensitive to the matter of bad checks, and I was pleased to be able to show her I'd inherited her caution.

The client in my first civil lawsuit also came from the Melody Room. He was a seventy-five-year-old cook who had been standing outside the restaurant one afternoon when a bundle of newspapers was thrown from a *Herald-Examiner* truck and hit him in the groin. His major complaint was that the injuries interfered with his sex life. The lawyers for the newspaper found it hard to believe that a man his age could have much of a sex life, but I convinced them his girl friends were ready to testify at the forthcoming trial. Eventually we settled the case out of court for $800.

In those first years, I took almost any kind of case I could get—personal injury, drunk driving, breach of contract, right-of-way, criminal, whatever. I hadn't decided on a field of specialization and anyway I didn't have enough experience to pursue one exclusively. Besides, I had an office to maintain and a landlord and secretary who expected to be paid regardless of the size or success of my practice.

From time to time since I started practice I've been involved in "cause" cases, but one that almost inundated me with clients at the outset of my career came as a result of a chance meeting with a former Army lieutenant colonel. During our conversation I mentioned I was an attorney and he told me he thought he needed one. He had held a rather high-level position in the guided missile program until he began suffering frequent bouts of illness which the Army couldn't diagnose. Finally, they decided his problems were psychosomatic and released him on a medical discharge but without a disability pension. At the time, he had had nineteen and a half years in the service, which left him just six months shy of retirement. After his discharge, civilian doctors discovered he was suffering from gallstones, which had gone undiagnosed for so long it was necessary to remove half his stomach. When I met him he was getting nowhere with his attempts to make the Army admit its responsibility.

Unable to find an expert on military law in Los Angeles, I wrote to Washington for a manual on how to proceed and then prepared a 125-page legal brief accompanied by more than fifty exhibits. Armed with all this evidence, I flew to Washington and presented the case. The size of our effort left the Army Board for Correction of Military Records nonplussed. It seems the usual approach was to write a letter outlining the problem and wait for the board to get around to acting on it. Few lawyers bothered giving full legal preparation to this sort of claim and seldom did anyone appear in person before the board.

In our case, the Army ordered some further medical tests on the colonel at Letterman General Hospital in San Francisco. When the results came in, they set a hearing and I again went to Washington, accompanied by my client, to argue his position. The Army ruled in his favor and ordered he be given more than $100,000 in back pay and allowances, plus full retirement rights.

Subsequently, my office was deluged with requests for military claims representation from individuals and veterans groups from all over the state. There was no possible way for me to handle them all, even if I had wanted to become a military claims specialist. And although military law would have been a promising specialty in which to practice, the courts which hear such cases are in Washington, D.C., and I would either have had to move there or spend most of my time on planes flying back and forth. Being too much of a Californian for that, I ended up referring those who contacted me to a Washington law firm that specialized in such cases and went back to the practice of California law.

Even in the earliest days I had a number of domestic relations cases, including divorces, custody problems, and one rather widely publicized and spectacular "contributing to the delinquency of a minor" case, which stemmed from what was actually a custody issue over control of Beverly Aadland, blonde seventeen-year-old paramour of the late actor Errol Flynn. She had been taken into custody after a twenty-one-year-old stuntman named William ("Billy the Kid") Stanciu was shot to death in her apartment. Although the shooting was ruled accidental, the juvenile court ordered a hearing to determine if Beverly should be returned to her mother's custody or be placed in a foster home.

The District Attorney's office filed charges against Beverly's mother, Mrs. Florence Aadland, for "contributing to the delinquency of a minor," based on some rather compromising photographs that were made during a wild wine-drinking party at the Aadland residence and some secret tape recordings made by a former Flynn employee at the D.A.'s request.

I represented Florence Aadland. She was an extraordinary and uncontrollable personality whose aim in life was to see her daughter become a show business success. The courtroom proceedings were frequently stormy, and one time she was ejected from her own trial after she had interrupted a witness and started a wild shouting match. Once, to stop another outburst, I actually kicked her under the counsel table—hard. There was a *thunk*. She didn't seem to feel it and went right on talking. I kicked again—again *thunk,* and still no reaction from Florence. Afterwards I discovered why—I had been kicking her artificial leg.

Although I argued that many of the photographs had been posed and taken when Mrs. Aadland was unconscious and that most state witnesses were testifying under threats that bordered on blackmail, we lost the case. The party pictures and tape recordings, which wouldn't be admissible evidence under today's legal standards, were just too damning. Mrs. Aadland was found guilty and sentenced to eighty days in jail.

The sentence was vacated, however, after the Juvenile Court placed Beverly in the custody of a minister and his wife recommended by Florence. The guardians later booked Beverly into a New York nightclub, and she had a brief career as a singer before marrying soon after she turned eighteen. Sadly, Florence died shortly before Beverly made her debut and was thus deprived of seeing her dreams for Beverly fulfilled.

At this point, I was still enjoying the challenges and the experiences of the various cases coming my way, but hadn't yet faced the one in which every aspiring trial lawyer ultimately longs to take part—a real matter of life or death, a murder case.

CHAPTER THREE

All the Way to the Supreme Court

The tear-stained face of the aging woman sitting stiffly in front of my desk bore the marks of a life that had experienced more than its share of suffering. "Mr. Mitchelson," she said, "Please help my boy. He's not a murderer."

Mrs. Farena Douglas had been referred to me by her sister, who was a maid at the home of one of my clients. Her son, William, an unemployed ex-Navy man, had been charged with murdering a policeman and was now in the jail ward of L.A. County General Hospital recovering from bullet wounds received during the incident.

Although the weapon used in the slaying did indeed belong to Bill, the gunning down of Sergeant Gene Nash had actually been done by another person at the scene, a paroled convict named Benny Will Meyes. Despite the fact that Nash had identified Meyes as his slayer before he died, Bill was also being charged, under a California law that makes anyone involved in a crime resulting in homicide equally guilty.

Bill had almost been killed himself in the furious gun battle that erupted when Nash and his partner burst into the bedroom of Bill's apartment, and the location of Bill's wounds rather strongly supported his story that he was crouched next to the bed with his rear in the air when the detective began firing. Indeed, as I pointed out in court later, the first doctor who examined him pronounced him dead at the scene. However, the police claimed Bill and Meyes were both members of a gang of armed robbers who were using Bill's apartment for a meeting place. Early reports even indicated Bill was "flushed" from the closet where he crawled to hide after the shooting started. But Bill had no criminal record and after our first meeting at the hospital jail ward I was totally convinced of his innocence.

At that time in early 1959, my practice had begun to grow, both in volume and prominence of clients. But, as I said, I had never been involved in a murder trial and decided to take the case. I wanted the chance to test my legal ability in the big arena. The desire to challenge authority is probably part of every lawyer's make-up but, in addition, there's the good feeling that comes from being able to champion the underdog. Bill's case was rich in all elements: he was black, he was poor, and the authorities had branded him a cop killer.

I really didn't expect the case to bring a fee or any particular recognition, but I was wrong on both counts. Though poor, Mrs. Douglas was proud and honest, and she paid the entire fee in a long series of monthly payments. And the recognition that came a few years later as a result of the case was entirely unexpected and out of all proportion to what I imagined when I first decided to accept it.

Both Bill and Meyes were tried together, with Meyes being represented by Paul Breckenridge, a capable public defender. In the six-week trial, the District Attorney claimed that Meyes opened fire when the two policemen burst into the room and that Bill, who was standing outside the closet door, was wounded by the stricken Nash. Bill and Meyes testified they were in the back bedroom when they heard the policemen in the front room. Bill said he became frightened when he heard the officers in the front, and tried to crawl under the bed. Meyes testified Nash started shooting first when the police entered the room and that he fired back in self-defense, not knowing they were policemen.

In my final argument to the jury, I stressed that medical

testimony on the angle of the bullet which pierced his rectum and almost killed Bill supported the veracity of his story.

In closing, I argued, "Three times Bill Douglas came close to death—when the sergeant shot him, when the doctor pronounced him dead at the scene, and later at the hospital when he almost died again. Three times God chose to let him live. I ask you not to reverse that verdict."

But the jury couldn't agree on a verdict for either man, and a mistrial was declared. The District Attorney promptly decided to try them again. In the second trial the jury acquitted Bill, while Meyes was found guilty of second-degree murder.

Still the state wasn't ready to free Bill Douglas, and he and Meyes were charged with thirteen additional felonies stemming from the robbery investigation Nash was conducting at the time of the shooting. Among the charges were assault with a deadly weapon, armed robbery, and assault with intent to commit murder.

Once again the two were ordered to stand trial together, although Meyes was a convicted murderer with a long criminal record, while Bill had no record and had been acquitted of the same murder. This time, unfortunately, I was engaged in other trials and could not defend him.

Bill and Meyes were declared indigents, people too poor to hire a private lawyer, and a new deputy from the Los Angeles Public Defender's Office was assigned to defend them. Despite obvious conflicts of interests posed by the differences in circumstances and criminal backgrounds, a single deputy public defender was assigned to represent both men. When the trial opened, the public defender asked for a postponement on the grounds that he hadn't had time to prepare a defense. At the same time, Meyes and Bill requested that separate counsel be appointed because their individual interests were in conflict. Both motions were denied, and the trial was ordered to proceed. The two men then dismissed their public defender on the grounds that he was not prepared for trial, and they renewed their request that separate counsel be appointed. Again, the request was refused. The trial proceeded with both men standing "mute," which meant they refused to take any part in the proceedings other than to make repeated requests for the appointment of separate counsel. The trial ended with both being convicted and sentenced to long terms in prison.

Meyes, however, had become quite a good jailhouse lawyer over the years and managed to get an appeal started for himself and Bill. In those days, the California District Court of Appeals would look at the transcript of the trial, and under the so-called "discretionary rule" if it thought there was any merit to the issues being appealed, it would ask the county bar association to provide the indigents with a lawyer. Conversely, if the district court felt there were no meritorious issues, an indigent defendant was obliged to handle the appeal on his own—without the benefit of a lawyer. A defendant of means appealing his case would obviously not suffer from such lack of counsel.

Thus, there were two important issues involved in these cases: both men had been represented by the same (not separate) counsel at their original trial, and they had carried out their appeal unassisted by the expert services of an attorney. On this basis, Meyes carried their case up the appeals ladder—first to the California District Court of Appeals, then to the California Supreme Court.

When they lost at the state supreme court level, Farena Douglas once more asked for my help. I agreed to help Bill again because I strongly believed that the pair's constitutional rights had been disregarded. The Fourth Amendment to the Constitution entitles every defendant to equal protection under the law. The two men had been denied counsel on appeal, simply because they were too poor to pay for it. With the Douglas and Meyes case denied in the California District Appellate and Supreme Court, that left only the court of last resort—the United States Supreme Court. That prospect didn't provide us with too much hope, for that highest of judical tribunals is deluged with literally thousands of petitions for review of lower court decisions (called writs of certiorari) every year. Of necessity, the justices can select only a handful of them for consideration, and these are restricted to cases where a question of a broad constitutional principle of law is raised. But, to my gratification, in the spring of 1962 I learned that our case was accepted for review and that I would be arguing it.

Appellate hearings are completely different from trial courts, where lawyers often clash head on with witnesses and opposing counsel in a battle to establish the facts. It's in the appellate courts, however, that attorneys get down to practicing real law, because it is the law itself, its meaning and interpretation, that must be argued on appeal. All matters of fact are regarded as settled by the trial court (unless there is a clear abuse of discretion). But though the appellate court is where law is practiced, the U.S. Supreme Court is the place where law is made binding or at least redefined into new and different meanings.

I wasn't entirely confident that I was ready to appear before the highest court in the land, but there were two strong points in my favor. First, under Chief Justice Earl Warren the Supreme Court had shown greater concern for individual rights than had any other Supreme Court in our history. Second, my friend Burton Marks, an excellent appellate and constitutional lawyer, would be there as co-counsel representing Meyes.

Many hours of work went into preparing the case. The justices, who carefully study all cases before the hearing, are notorious for interrupting a lawyer's planned presentation to have him clarify points or questions of their own. The Court rules are very rigid, and we were each given a half hour to argue our side of the case, regardless of how many interruptions the Court made. We had agreed that Burt would take the first half hour, and I would cover the remaining points of our argument in the last thirty minutes. This meant that I would have to be thoroughly familiar with every point of our argument, since we couldn't be sure how many issues the justices would allow Burt to cover.

In October we flew to Washington to argue the case. There is something awesome about a Supreme Court session. After the lawyers take their places at the counsel table below the bench, there is the sudden appearance of the justices through the red drapes that hang between the massive marble columns in back of the bench. The impact is matched only by the justices equally abrupt departure at the end of the session—both events executed precisely on the scheduled minute.

I was still trying to get the lump out of my throat after that dramatic opening, when Chief Justice Earl Warren interrupted

Burt with a question—less than two minutes into his argument. My co-counsel had been trying to make a point we considered sequentially important, and he tried to sidetrack the Chief Justice's line of questioning by saying that I intended to cover it later in my part of the argument.

"In that case," the Chief Justice remarked dryly, "I suggest that Mr. Mitchelson discuss it now."

It took us both unawares, especially me. Mentally I was not ready, by at least twenty-eight minutes. But a suggestion from the bench is a command. Burt sat down and I stood up—much too quickly, clumsily knocking all the transcripts, books, and carefully arranged notes off the counsel table onto the floor. Mumbling a hasty "Excuse me!" I stooped to retrieve everything. In the deathly silence I tried to stay calm, at least on the outside, as I slowly and deliberately gathered up my materials and put them back on the table. I then started my argument, making a special effort to speak in a quiet, deliberate, conversational tone. But I barely had a chance to outline my plea when the questions started.

For the next fifty-seven minutes I tried to make my main legal points, and the ones Burt had intended to make, mostly by attempting to answer the Court's questions within the framework of the issues as we saw them. There were several different questions raised in the appeal, including whether Meyes and Douglas should have been provided with separate counsel at the trial court level, whether they intelligently waived their right to counsel when they dismissed their public defender, and whether as indigents they were entitled to appointed counsel for their appeal.

I thought the most important issue was the right for the two men to have separate counsel appointed for their trial. All the other questions seemed to hinge on that. If they had a right to separate counsel, I argued, they had the right to refuse to accept just one public defender, and in that case the trial court erred in refusing to delay the trial until both men had lawyers.

Chief Justice Warren asked why they should have been given separate lawyers. It was just the question I was waiting for, and I pounced on it because I had tried the murder case in which the pair had had separate counsel and received different verdicts. How, I responded, could the same lawyer argue that Douglas was innocent without inferring that Meyes was guilty? It was plain to me that the same lawyer couldn't adequately represent both men.

The justices showed a great deal of interest in the murder case, but as the questioning continued it became apparent that they were much more concerned with whether indigents had the right to appointed counsel for their appeals. I remember Justice Tom Clark (who ended up writing a dissenting opinion) expressing particular concern that a blanket guarantee of counsel would flood the courts with extra litigation.

Finally, the session ended and the case stood submitted. Neither Burt nor I had that feeling of victory or defeat which usually comes to a lawyer at some point in a trial. Weeks dragged by with no decision, and we concluded that the Court was having trouble making up its mind, which we interpreted as a good sign. Then, suddenly we were asked to come back and reargue the whole case—a rare action on the part of the Court.

The second hearing turned out to be a marathon session with the Court allowing us to argue an extra thirty minutes. In that hearing, which was held in January of 1963, we began to realize they had been holding our case as one of the companion cases in a series of landmark decisions on the rights of indigents to counsel. We knew our case had been chosen to deal specifically with the indigent's right to counsel on appeal, and so we tailored our main argument to that point. But the justices still showed a lot of interest in the Douglas-Meyes murder trial—which, I suppose, is why they gave us the extra time for argument.

The decision came down on March 18, 1963, with a 6-3 ruling in our favor to remand the case back to the California courts for further proceedings. As we expected, the decision was restricted to the issue of providing the poor with free counsel on appeal. The majority opinion, written by Justice William O. Douglas, called California's previous procedure an "invidious discrimination" which drew "an unconstitutional line between the rich and poor," because it forced the appellate court to "prejudge the merits of an appeal before it can even determine if counsel should be provided."

"Unless the barren pages of the record show an injustice has been committed," Justice Douglas wrote, "he [the indigent] is forced to go without a champion on appeal." He added that in cases where the record is unclear or the errors hidden, "the indigent has only the right to a meaningless ritual, while the rich man has a meaningful appeal."

Justice Clark, in his dissenting opinion, voiced his earlier concern about flooding the courts with extra litigation, charging that an "overwhelming" percentage of appeals filed with the High Court by poor people were "frivolous." He also stated that he thought giving indigents an absolute right to counsel on appeal was an "utter extravagance and waste of state funds." Justices John Harlan and Potter Stewart also dissented, writing that an unrestricted right to such counsel "can only lead to mischievous results" and defended the previous California system as a "reasonable step to guard against needless expense."

But the majority opinion was binding, and it struck down the California rule that left to the court the decision on appointing appeal cousel for the indigent. Our case, along with *Gideon* v. *Wainwright* and *Draper* v. *Washington,* became a landmark decision which guaranteed poor people the same legal rights at all judicial levels as the wealthy. (*Gideon* guaranteed counsel at the trial court level, and *Draper* guaranteed the poor a free transcript of trial proceedings for the appeal.)

Bill Douglas was later retried with his own separate counsel and convicted on some of the charges. He was sentenced to prison but was released some years later and has been in no further trouble. Meyes was also sentenced on some counts and eventually released.

My participation in this Supreme Court decision added a new dimension to my practice. I was asked to be guest lecturer at various law schools and appeared on radio and television talk shows as a "constitutional lawyer" (where I felt obligated to point out that one Supreme Court case does not a constitutional lawyer make).

One of the most valuable results of the case was psychological. Probably one of the most important assets a lawyer—especially a young lawyer—can have is the confidence that he is capable of defending his client's cause. That confidence stays with him for a long time when that client's case has been successfully defended in the highest court in the land.

CHAPTER FOUR

"Let's Kill All the Lawyers"

I first met Pamela Mason at a Christmas party. She was an intelligent woman who was truly liberated long before that status became organized. At the time we were introduced, someone mentioned my Supreme Court case. It not only failed to impress her, it provided her with an excuse to launch into a sharp-tongued tirade against the whole legal profession. Her favorite quotation, she let me know, was from Shakespeare's *Henry VI:* "The first thing we do, let's kill all the lawyers."

The reason for her acerbity soon became clear. Pamela was then in the middle of a marital battle with James Mason, the handsome and urbane actor who had been her husband for twenty-one years, and she had just dismissed her second set of lawyers. I learned that part of her bitterness stemmed from the fact that her lawyers had negotiated pretrial fees with James's lawyers and informed her of their actions only after the fact. I tried to explain that it was normal practice for attorneys to agree on a fee to be paid by the husband prior to the trial so that the wife could be properly represented, particularly if she didn't have the means to pay for competent lawyers herself. It was a procedure that had developed because the husband traditionally managed community funds, and so it was really a *protection* for wives.

But Pamela refused to accept this explanation. "It's a sell-out," she snapped. "How can they really be on my side and fight for me when they're taking money from him?" In the future, she told me, she intended to represent herself. After all, she said, "I love myself, so I can't be bribed. Besides I can't do any worse than the rest, and I won't be wasting thousands of dollars out of our community property on lawyers' fees."

When the party ended, I doubted I would ever see her again, but a week or so later she called and asked me to be a guest on her extraordinarily outspoken talk show. I suspected she planned to use me as a straight man for public denunciation of the legal profession—and I wasn't disappointed. Still, I think I surprised her somewhat during the course of the show when she asked me why lawyers made wills so complicated and why there were so many whereases, wherefores, and wherefroms. I could have given her the lengthy legal explanation she probably expected, telling her that precise language is necessary to make these instruments binding. I chose instead to give her a short and simple example. I told her that the shortest will on record, upheld by a probate court, consisted of three words, "All to mother." (I didn't tell her that I had accidentally run across this fact from the *Guinness Book of World Records* just before the show was taped.) After that, Pamela's attack on lawyers noticeably diminished.

From our conversation, I suspected Pamela knew I wanted to represent her in the case against James, and that she used my guest appearance on her show to test my performance. For a young lawyer, becoming attorney number three was a most challenging and exciting opportunity on several levels.

Since Mason was living in Switzerland and had most of his corporate assets in Liechtenstein, there were complex legal and jurisdictional issues. In addition, there was the matter of the division of a large amount of money and property. Pamela reminded me that her share—estimated at over a million dollars—was rightfully her money to begin with. Besides, the Masons were popular with the American public and the film community, and since it was threatened that Mason's lawyers would countercharge Pamela, there was the promise of a sensational public battle if the case went to trial. It would have been unnatural for an attorney not to want to be involved.

During the next couple of weeks, Pamela called and asked me to handle some minor legal matters that did not involve her divorce action. I was careful not to solicit the case and she continued to ignore everyone's advice, including the old maxim "He who represents himself has a fool for a client"—the most valuable advice anyone can give a person involved in a divorce action where money, property, or children are involved. Her standard retort to any suggestion that it might be wiser to find a new lawyer rather than represent herself was, "All you lawyers hate the idea of my depriving some fellow lawyer of a fat fee."

Friends told her that in hiring Jake Ehrlich her husband was represented by one of the most prominent lawyers on the West Coast and that she was pitting herself against a man whose legal fame had inspired the television series *Sam Benedict*. But she continued to let the paperwork and complications pile up, until one day she remarked, "If I ever decided to hire another lawyer, it would have to be on my terms. I won't have him negotiating for fees with James's lawyers."

I told her the alternative would be for the lawyer to apply to the court and have the judge set the fee.

"I won't have that either," she countered. "If I have to trust a lawyer, then he has to trust me. I'll set the fee, and I'll pay him. Do you know a lawyer who'd accept those terms?"

"There's only one that I can think of," I answered.

When she finally got around to it, it was as simple as that. "Would you represent me?" she asked.

Damn right I would, I thought—or should I, I wondered, trying not to think about the fact that it would be without a retainer or guaranteed fee and that I was placing myself at the mercy of a determined woman who could, and would, dismiss me if I failed to measure up.

"I'd be delighted," I answered finally. It was a calculated risk, but one worth taking, and I quickly settled down to putting the decision behind me, and the work before me.

My initial review of the Mason file indicated that the case would revolve more around untangling the maze of complications that surrounded the Masons' financial affairs than around any of the sensational charges on either side. However, the fact that Ehrlich could field a first, second, and probably a third team, if necessary, put my one-lawyer office at a decided disadvantage. Ehrlich had relatively unlimited funds, manpower, and time to devote to the case, and Pamela's conditions put me under somewhat of a strain. I'd developed a busy, though not overly lucrative practice. Without advance fees or expenses, I had to work on her case between the routine legal affairs that kept my own home and office together. But I was determined to make the most of this case, no matter what it took.

When I took over, we were less than three months from the scheduled trial date, which put me under heavy pressure to familiarize myself immediately with all the issues. Out of necessity, I developed a rather peculiar work habit, which has since become permanent. Every night for about three months before the trial, I arose at 2 A.M. and worked on the case for at least three hours. Without constant telephone calls, client appointments, and other inevitable interruptions, I had the equivalent of a full day's work done by the time my office opened.

Although I was confident that California law would ultimately control the issues of this case, I had to familiarize myself with the laws of Switzerland, where Mason claimed residence, and of Liechtenstein, where he had formed a corporation. During the day I'd call on appraisers, tax consultants, and foreign legal experts for answers to my questions and then review their opinions. It was time well spent. It helped me determine that Pamela's estimate in the community assets was overly conservative. Also, I decided it would be in both Pamela's and Mason's best interests to settle the case out of court rather than their going through the agony of a full-blown trial. That prospect disappointed me a little, since it wouldn't be the same challenge as trying the case in court. But, after all, it was the Masons' estate at stake, not mine, so I was easy to convince.

Though I suspected her pride had been hurt, Pamela was woman enough not to be personally vindictive toward her husband, even though the two Jane Does originally named in the suit filed by

Pamela turned out to have different last names. There were, of course, the two children to be considered. And though the marriage was no longer viable, she still had enormous respect and affection for James, so there was no great conflict on her part.

As for Ehrlich, his law firm had a substantial head start, and he was willing to talk settlement practically from the moment I entered the case. But I was determined not to discuss settlement at all until I knew what I was talking about. My reluctance to negotiate gave me a decided psychological advantage, since almost all litigants want their cases settled rather than tried. When a lawyer deliberately refuses or puts off settlement discussions with the other side, he often creates a sense of insecurity on their part. "Do they have some evidence we've overlooked?" they ask themselves. My insistence on negotiating with Ehrlich directly, since he had the ultimate word in any important decisions, I hoped would add to any sense of insecurity they might already have.

Two weeks before we were scheduled to go to trial, I had compiled a list of about forty prominent persons in the entertainment world who were friends of Pamela and James and whom I felt would be useful witnesses in the forthcoming trial. I prepared subpoenas for each of them and sent my process servers into the field to serve them. From my own experience in serving subpoenas, I knew the result that could be expected—immediate panic. The deluge of telephone calls to both myself and Mason's lawyers proved I was right as one potential witness after another implored us to keep them out of the trial. The effect was precisely what I wanted. My explanation to all was an expression of polite regret that we were forced into a potentially nasty trial that we didn't want, but we had no other choice—unless, of course, we could settle the case.

Meanwhile, the eve of the trial was almost upon us and we were yet to have our first negotiating session. Finally, late on the Friday afternoon before the Monday trial date, Ehrlich called from San Francisco to ask if I would meet with his team over the weekend to see if we could find a way to avoid a courtroom showdown. He assured me that they had serious proposals to discuss, and that he personally would also be coming down with his associates. I agreed to meet them in my office Saturday morning. At ten o'clock three members of the negotiating team walked in, but Ehrlich was not among them. The legendary San Francisco barrister chose instead to stay in his Beverly Wilshire Hotel suite, across the street from my office. However, his associates told me he was only a telephone call away if any decisions had to be made that they were not authorized to make.

Ehrlich's negotiating team included an attorney named Luther Avery, a meticulous, articulate man in a vest who proved to be a tough-minded expert on taxes and finances. During negotiations we had no trouble agreeing which assets were community property, and I had the feeling for the first time that our chances of working it all out were good.

The problem came over the value of these assets and some questionable quasi-community property, and the battle went on all day, all night, and into the early hours of Sunday. When stalemate threatened, I said, "Call Ehrlich—you said he's only a phone call away." We actually called him several times, and almost every time, some form of concession resulted. It turned out the old master's strategy of aloofness was working to my advantage.

Finally, with throats and tempers getting raw, we agreed to recess until Sunday afternoon. We needed the time for sleep and strategy sessions, they with Ehrlich and me with Pamela. In our meeting I told Pamela I was mildly optimistic about a settlement but that she should still prepare herself for a court appearance on Monday. She in turn gave me something new to work with, if it became necessary. If an agreeable property division could be worked out, she said, she would waive alimony and accept their formula for putting part of the child-support money in trust for the children.

Late Sunday afternoon, back at the negotiating table, both sides played it close to Avery's vest. Throughout the night, he and I discovered that we could compromise on point after point. I kept a running account of the assets that we agreed were community property, and long before we finished I knew the amount would give Pamela more than the $1 million she originally felt she was entitled to. Realizing there were no more points to be gained, I agreed to waive Pamela's alimony, and accepted the child-support formula.

I read from my notes, summarized the points, and then asked, "Gentlemen, is that our agreement?"

"Agreement, hell!" one of Ehrlich's attorneys said. "It's an unconditional surrender!"

The war was over.

At 3 A.M. I called my secretary out of bed to start typing up the agreement for signature before court convened, then headed for Pamela's house to get her approval. She was waiting in her study with the martini I had told her I would need in order to go through—for the second time within a few hours—a review of the full negotiating process and its benefits for her.

When I explained the details, she was speechless—but not for long. She again ripped apart the legal profession in general. But it was concern for her husband that prompted it. "Poor James," she said, "how could they do that to him?" Mason, however, didn't see it in that light. The next day in the courthouse corridor, when asked about the settlement, he remarked, "It's only a flea bite."

She also agreed the fee I was at last free to name was too small, and raised it. As a bonus, Pamela, in a moment of enthusiasm, promised to ship a Rolls-Royce from England on her next trip there as special compensation for my services.

She insisted on driving me down to the courthouse for the final formalities in her own Silver Cloud Rolls so I'd get used to riding in one.

The court corridors were packed with spectators and media people who had come to hear the anticipated sensational testimony of the forty witnesses. When Pamela finished the mild statements required to establish "mental cruelty," the press had nothing left to focus on but the amount of the settlement.

"How'd you do it?" a woman reporter asked Pamela.

Pamela put her hand on my arm and said, "I got a lawyer who worked very hard and in whom I believed."

That very public accolade was worth far more to me than the Rolls-Royce, which, incidentally, never arrived.

CHAPTER FIVE

The Indignity of Divorce

The New York divorce of famed lyricist Allen Jay Lerner and his pretty Parisian wife, Micheline, is an almost classic study of what happens when bitterness and emotion overcome all else. In their highly publicized case, the acrimonious aspects intensified when the couple chose as their champions a pair of supercapable attorneys whose own legal feuding had reached the personal level.

New York is a state without community property laws and, at the time, adultery was the only ground for divorce. Lerner's fame plus the storybook background of the couple's jet-set romance and the situation's potential for bloodletting made hope of civilized conduct improbable, and the added weight of legal rivalry made it impossible.

I came into the picture after the battle was already joined. Micheline had come to California with the Lerners' six-year-old son, Michel, where a friend of Pamela Mason's recommended that she talk to me. The people involved immediately made me interested in the case, although I was concerned by the fact that I would become co-counsel with Roy Cohn.

Cohn had become a public figure when, in the early fifties, he took on the United States Army in the famed Army-McCarthy hearings as associate special counsel of Senator Joseph McCarthy.

He was well known as a blunt man with a rather abrasive personality who practiced law like a bulldozer. He had a reputation for single-minded trust in his own intelligence, ability, and tactics. And—as I suspected even before we met—he found it difficult to be a team player, especially with an attorney not of his own choosing.

Lerner's attorney was the equally famed and formidable Louis Nizer, whose court record was well known, dealing with numerous theater, motion picture, and television personalities, and was also the author of the bestselling book, *My Life in Court.* The two lawyers had recently generated headlines by battling the Mexican divorce of New York multimillionaire Louis Rosenstiel (of Schenley Whiskey) up to the state's highest court. Cohn had won, and the Lerner case had therefore taken on the overtones of a rematch.

The Lerners were as colorful as their lawyers. Alan Lerner was the immensely talented lyricist who had written one musical hit after another, including *Brigadoon, My Fair Lady, Camelot,* and the love story, *Gigi,* which he created expressly for Micheline. She was the daughter of a French general, had studied at the Sorbonne, and had been admitted to the French bar at age twenty, becoming that nation's youngest lawyer. A chic, blonde gamine, she claimed descent from Napoleon and exhibited some of that Corsican's strong-willed imperiousness.

My first meeting with Micheline was in September, 1964, at the Beverly Hills Hotel bungalow where she and her son had taken up residence. She told me she had decided to become a California resident and would need a local attorney.

Micheline's immediate problem was a New York contempt of court hearing over her refusal to bring the boy back East. She claimed that Lerner had agreed they could stay in California pending trial of the divorce, and she had enrolled Michel in an exclusive school in Beverly Hills. Lerner, however, contended he gave permission only for a visit, and demanded the boy be returned immediately.

There were other problems involving what Lerner considered Micheline's "extravagant" expenses and Nizer's very realistic fear that her change of residence was the first move in an effort to shift the divorce action to California, where community property laws could be evoked. That was precisely what she had in mind, but we couldn't coax Lerner into the state to serve the summons necessary to make him subject to the California courts' jurisdiction. Nizer had warned Lerner not to set foot in California under any circumstances, although it prevented the lyricist from personally seeing not only Michel but two daughters by his previous marriage to motion picture actress Nancy Olson. To make sure that Micheline responded to the contempt action, Lerner cut off her rather substantial temporary support payments and telegraphed the Beverly Hills Hotel that he would no longer be responsible for his wife's bills (which at the time came to over $29,000).

After careful review of the file, I flew to New York for a meeting with Cohn. It came off much as I expected. He was reserved, polite, and slightly patronizing as he accepted my honest compliments on his work on the case. When he said he would be happy to consider any suggestions I might make, I took him at face value and began to outline what I thought would be needed in the way of pleadings and affidavits from California for the upcoming contempt hearing. My ideas made virtually no impression on him, however, and it soon became clear that his definition of co-counsel differed significantly from mine.

Back in California I explained the problem to Micheline, and her legal training proved an asset to me. On my next trip East, I took with me the one thing that could force cooperation from a heavyweight lawyer of Cohn's temperament—authority to replace him with another attorney if I thought it necessary.

Since he was a tough, capable trial lawyer with a first-class record, I certainly didn't want to remove him, but I had no intention of carrying his lawbooks around. I put the matter to him in the same hard-nosed manner he would have used if our roles had been reversed. Roy apparently wanted to fight Nizer more than he wanted to fight me, and from that point on we found it possible to work together.

Cohn's almost contemptuous attitude toward people he considered weaker or less smart was rather poignantly revealed the morning of the Lerner custody hearing. In New York, judges conduct pretrial hearings in divorce actions by reading written affidavits rather than hearing in-person testimony. That system has certain advantages, especially in a long-distance battle like the Lerner case. It's much easier and less expensive, for instance, to obtain a sworn affidavit than to bring someone clear across country to testify as a witness. We had no more intention of bringing Micheline or Michel into New York than Nizer had of letting Lerner go to California, but for some reason Lerner expected the boy in the courtroom when he came to the hearing. He was a small, slender man dressed in Saville Row clothes, and his face was pale and drawn. He paced the courtroom and kept glancing about agitatedly. Finally, he asked, "Where's Michel?"

"Why he's right here under the bench," Cohn deadpanned, and called, "Come on out, Michel."

Lerner bent down to look under the bench, and Cohn looked at me with a smirk. I felt sorry for Lerner, who, after all, was just a father hoping to see his son and who didn't much care if he looked foolish in the process.

Before I entered the case, the battle of affidavits had been heavy in both volume and vitriol. Lerner, for example, had filed one by his family physician stating Michel's welfare required him to be with his father. Then Micheline obtained an opinion from another pediatrician stating separation from the father would do the boy no harm.

Both lawyers also made ample use of their clients' filings to hurl barbs at each other. Cohn, for instance, took on both Lerner and Nizer in one affidavit filed over Micheline's signature that stated:

> It is clear from defendant's and his attorney's conduct that they are using the court only for the purpose of harassing the plaintiff. . . . Defendant's and his attorney's continual vacillation, and their knowingly making of applications, under totally false allegations, clearly show conduct toward the plaintiff which can only be characterized as "Gaslight Treatment" [referring to a classic movie, *Gaslight*, about a man's attempts to drive his wife insane].

Nizer, with his gift for old-fashioned prose, fired back an answering document over Lerner's signature:

Mr. Roy M. Cohn, unencumbered by any personal knowledge of the facts, launches an attack upon me which is as shocking for the bitterness of his intemperate language as it is for the utter falsity of his factual assertions. . . . I am constrained to answer the more flagrant of his fabrications lest the slightest inference be drawn from silence in the face of such unmitigated falsehoods.

Despite an abundance of documentation pro and con, the written record upheld Lerner's contention that he had given his wife permission only to "visit" California. Under these circumstances, I realized we would need some pretty potent arguments to convince the court it should overlook Micheline's apparent violation of its orders.

About the only thing that can convince a judge in such circumstances is a strong appeal that it served the best interests of the child, and since a picture is supposed to be worth a thousand words, I decided to try the graphic approach. We hired a photographer who, using long-range telephoto lenses so Michel wouldn't know he was being photographed, put together a photo essay depicting a happy, healthy child in the settings of home, school, and play. These candid shots, backed by affidavits from teachers, nurse, and others proved to be the turning point. The judge ruled Michel could stay in California—at least until the school year ended.

With the custody-contempt issue out of the way and Micheline's temporary support reaffirmed (though on more modest terms), the way was clear for the main bout—the divorce trial. In this, both sides should have recognized their own vulnerability, but instead each relentlessly pressed forward in the search for evidence, which finally resulted in massive overkill. Hordes of private detectives were hired on both coasts. Some spied on Lerner, some on Micheline and Michel, some were even employed to spy on the spies. Detailed dossiers were compiled on both parties, with names and photos of all visitors and round-the-clock timetables listing every arrival and departure. One group of detectives followed Michel around and made detailed charts of his movements in order to develop a plan of spiriting him out of California and return him to New York. Another group consisted of Howard Hughes' security people who maintained watch over the business tycoon's unused bungalow next to Micheline's at the Beverly Hills Hotel. They moonlighted for Lerner. Later, they moonlighted for us.

While much of this Keystone Kop activity was going on, I was commuting even more frequently to New York for settlement conferences, which often wound up with me trying to keep Nizer and Cohn from going at each other.

The Lerners, too, preserved an acerbic relationship, with Michel often caught in the middle. Pettiness ruled. Once we had to obtain a court order to get the boy's winter clothing shipped to California. Another time when Michel needed dental work, Lerner refused to let Micheline's dentist touch his son. She said no dentist of Lerner's choice would work on her son's teeth. A Solomonic compromise was reached by having his choice and her choice pick a third dentist for the boy.

The trial began in early March. We filed into Manhattan's aging stone courthouse one bleak morning, surrounded by reporters and photographers, who noisily followed us from the front-step colonnades to the door of the high-ceilinged courtroom. Inside, the spectator section was packed from wall to dingy wall with people who had come to watch the high and mighty carve each other up. Now the people who had avidly followed the Lerners' whirlwind romance and marriage were watching the relationship crumble with equal fascination. And the stage was set to give them an earful.

The more scandalous issues had already been widely reported by the press, which chronicled them from the case pleadings—the formal written complaints, charges, and statements which are public records. Both partners charged and countercharged each other with almost every conceivable kind of conduct: adultery, association with people of questionable character, refusal to cohabit—none of which bore any resemblance to the marriage which had begun as if it were truly "made in heaven."

On the first day of the trial Micheline was the first witness. A hush fell over the spectators, who had endured hours of lawyers wrangling over preliminary motions and introduction of various exhibits. In response to our questioning, Micheline described, in her bubbly French accent, aspects of their sex life that made the late afternoon headlines even before we got out of court.

But Nizer had his counterstroke. While cross-examining her, he suddenly whipped out a small, red-leather book. "Is this your diary?" he asked.

Micheline hadn't told us about the diary and apparently had no idea that it was missing and in Lerner's hands. Cohn and I objected long and vigorously on every ground we could think of, but the best we could do was to stall things until court was adjourned and we had a chance to find out what it might contain.

The diary was potential dynamite in Nizer's hands. The intensely personal account, written in French, was laced with reveries, daydreams, and romantic fantasies. And far too much of it concerned a young man named Peter.

Nizer wasted no time getting to the heart of the diary when court resumed. "Did you write that you wanted a lover, handsome and young?" he asked Micheline.

"Yes, because I was disgusted with my husband. . . . He advised me to take a lover."

"A lover, beautiful and young?"

"A woman thinks such things." Micheline became sullen.

"What did you mean when you wrote 'One has to defrost Peter constantly, and I get enough of that'?"

"He was often sad and morose."

"And when you wrote 'He comes after dinner and I have two husbands instead of one'?"

"I enjoyed his company. We had many of the same interests." Micheline's face was flushed and her eyes full of tears.

"When Alan was out in California, didn't Peter occupy Alan's bed and wear his clothes?"

"I swear that is a lie. I loved Peter only as a friend."

Sitting at the counsel table, Lerner looked ill. Even Nizer's bland composure was forced. The only people who seemed to be enjoying the scene were the courtroom spectators themselves. It disturbed me to think that we had a legal system that forced two people to savagely strip each other of all dignity, just to dissolve a contract both wanted to end.

"What did you mean when you wrote, 'Marriage is a prison and I want to get out of it'?" Nizer pushed on.

"It was the truth at the time. It was the way I felt sometimes."

The questioning ground on, through entry after damning entry, until Nizer was finished and we had the opportunity for reexamination.

"Did your husband ever say he had the money, power, and influence to get custody of Michel?" Cohn asked.

"He said that . . . and I told him the child is my whole life, and that if he took him away I would kill myself. And I would."

Finally, the awful day ended. It was Friday, and the judge decided he had heard enough. He called us to the bench and in no uncertain terms let us know he felt the proceedings had plunged to such a low level they sullied the whole judicial process. All parties, he insisted, must settle the case by morning. Since neither side really wanted to continue what had been going on for the past few days, we negotiated all night and finally agreed on a settlement a half hour before court reconvened on Monday.

Obviously, with the threat of the character-searing public trial as the catalyst for negotiations, the Lerner divorce was the kind of case that should have gone to negotiated settlement very early on. Ever since, I've been partial to negotiated settlements, which avoid such open battle in court and so often leave participants as battlefield casualties. Certainly the Lerners might have saved themselves a great deal of hurt and public humiliation had there been less animosity and battle of the ego.

It was agreed both lawsuits would be withdrawn. Micheline would have custody of the boy, a cash settlement, and a Nevada divorce. The only remaining task was to divide the furnishings and art objects of their three-story town house. That lot fell to me because Nizer, Lerner, and Cohn couldn't stand to be in the same room with each other. This task (which took over a week) brought the only bright spot of the sad saga as far as I was concerned. One day I arrived early. Lerner, a gracious host who had become less hostile now that the legal proceedings were over, sat down at a piano (which was disputed property) and played most of the *Camelot* score for me. This led him to recall his visits to the White House when John F. Kennedy was president. And he wistfully concluded, "You know, Camelot doesn't last forever."

CHAPTER SIX

The Celebrity Divorce

"Some of the greatest love affairs I've known have involved one actor—unassisted," Wilson Mizner, Broadway and Hollywood wit, once wrote. Groucho Marx, in my opinion, is one of the world's funniest men. But his former wives do not see it that way. His first wife, after twenty-two years, said: "The marriage was a big joke." The second, after only five years, said: "It wasn't funny." And from representing his third wife, Eden, I learned that her relationship with Groucho also was sometimes no laughing matter.

It started when I got back to my office late one afternoon and found a message for me to call a Mrs. Marx. Thinking it was my aunt, who has the same last name, and that I could call her later at home, I almost left without returning the call. But the number on the message pad was not familiar, which puzzled me, and so I returned the call.

The phone was answered by Dee, Eden's sister, whom I'd met at a party once and who had persuaded Eden to call me. Eden, it turned out, had fled to Dee's home after finally deciding she had endured more insults and indignities than she could bear. She wanted to discuss divorce, and Dee wanted her to do it immediately. I agreed to meet with them at Dee's place in Beverly Hills.

Many lawyers are reluctant to make house calls. They believe that clients should be interviewed in an office, where diplomas on the wall and law books on the shelves underline the fact that you are there to talk business. Discussions at someone's home, no matter how serious, have certain social overtones. However, because celebrity and show business people often make such peculiar demands and are sometimes reluctant to being seen in public buildings, I find it necessary to violate the office-conference rule from time to time.

Eden, a one-time elegant fashion model who had become the third Mrs. Marx, turned out to be as shy in her sister's library as she always seemed to be in public. I suppose after seventeen years of being a somewhat unwilling "straight man" (woman) for an unrivaled master of the put-down, she had developed a knack for being unobtrusive, at least verbally. In fact, Dee did most of the talking during that first hour's discussion of the tribulations of life with Groucho, while Eden mainly nodded in agreement.

In the movies and on television, Groucho is a leering, little man with a big cigar and an old-fashioned cutaway coat who makes the ridiculous sublimely funny. As the great nonconformist who blows cigar smoke in the establishment's eye, Groucho is devastating. But this humor is unreal, impersonal, and only funny when it is aimed at targets that deserve it. Unfortunately, I learned from Eden, that the movie makeup almost never came off.

The two had met while Eden (born Edna), a struggling actress in her early twenties from Bell, California, was touring the set of Groucho's *A Girl in Every Port*. Despite the thirty-seven-years difference in their ages, a romance blossomed. Having caught the eye and affections of a man personifying fame, wealth, and luxury, Eden took it all as a true Cinderella story, even though the Prince Charming was sometimes considerably less than charming. Indeed, Eden plunged into marriage with little concern for the danger signs that were indicated by Groucho's two previous marital experiences. Now, after years of living in Groucho's shadow, of having her ego flattened and her personality subdued to virtual nonexistence, Eden had become part of that shadow—and little else.

Eden's list of mental cruelties later detailed in the court papers was long and varied. She told how Groucho complained loudly that she didn't know how to run a house whenever friends or members of her family came to dinner. He constantly reminded her of what he considered her "humble" origins, once breaking into a conversation she was having with Dee about a current play with the acid remark that "I suppose you two broads from Bell know more about show business than I do!"

When they were out together he frequently made a point of ignoring her, sometimes for whole evenings. Parties at home were worse; if things weren't going right, he would shout, "Hey, hostess! Where's the dinner? Boy, you're some hostess!" or other remarks calculated to put her down in front of their guests.

The final straw came at Chasen's Restaurant in Hollywood, where the Marxes were members of a small dinner party. Groucho was telling one of his endless stories when Eden made the mistake of interrupting him. Forgetting he was supposed to be a funnyman, Groucho turned and snapped, "Who the hell do you think you are? You may think you're Mrs. Groucho Marx, but remember that you're just plain Edna Higgens from Bell, California. . . . And don't you ever forget it!" Apparently the message got across, for Eden fled the restaurant in tears.

I told Eden she seemed to have ample grounds for a divorce and that if she decided to sue I would be willing to represent her, but that she should make certain that she really wanted to go forward with the case. She thought about it for a minute, then turned to her sister, and said rather sadly, "It's been a lousy marriage, and it's not getting any better."

But it was Dee who asked, "How soon can we get started?"

"Right now, if you wish," I responded, looking at Eden.

She smiled wistfully. "Now that I've decided, I guess I'd better not wait."

I called my secretary (who was becoming accustomed to my nocturnal habits), and shortly after midnight Eden signed the papers in my office.

Despite Eden's obvious hesitancy and indecision, I had sound tactical reasons for moving as fast as possible. I felt that she stood to benefit more if her case was tried before California's new 1970 "no-fault" divorce law went into effect and eliminated the possibility of a "wronged" party being awarded a greater share of the community assets. We had to obtain a trial date prior to the coming new year, when the new law would become effective. Actually, I hoped we wouldn't have to try the case under either the old or new law and that a reasonable settlement could be obtained.

I had also considered Groucho's overbearing nature and knew I'd need every possible psychological advantage just to stay even. Consequently, I arranged with my process server to make certain the divorce papers were served on Groucho early the next morning, before he had had any warning. Because Eden told me a servant would answer the door, I told the process server to say he had a special delivery package from the NBC Studios, where Groucho's *You Bet Your Life* shows were taped.

Groucho appeared at the door wearing his well-known sideways beanie and was handed the divorce papers. Included in the complaint were Eden's charges that he ridiculed her in front of relatives, guests, and servants; was prone to hostile and abusive moods; had an uncontrollable temper; had even struck her on New Year's Eve 1967. This last charge brought instant outrage, I learned a few hours later, when Groucho's lawyer called to acknowledge service of the papers. He said Groucho was terribly hurt by the charge. "Besides, she's bigger than he is and stronger than he is and he's scared as hell of her," the lawyer insisted.

As usual in long marriages where a lot of property is involved, it boiled down to a matter of discovering the location and amount of assets Groucho controlled. He had many kinds of property in many different parts of the country, and it kept me on the move gathering records and figures and developing information from potential witnesses in New York and other Eastern and Midwestern cities. He had invested heavily in stocks, bonds, and other securities during their seventeen years of marriage, and I ended up with mountains of records from bankers and brokers.

To expedite things, I decided to take Groucho's deposition early. Depositions are out-of-court examinations of witnesses or parties taken under oath and recorded by a shorthand reporter and later filed with the court. The attorney for the party being deposed is present and almost always gives his client the same advice that he give him if he is to testify in court—if possible, answer all questions yes or no, and never volunteer anything.

Depositions are supposed to be primary tools for "pretrial discovery," the term used to describe the processes for gathering relevant information before trial, but Groucho's deposition hearing in my office turned into an exciting, almost exhilarating sort of private "command" performance. His attorney was equally amused but hoped we wouldn't have the last laugh.

Groucho stalked into the room with the same extended-leg, knees-high, comic swagger that has been his trademark, and glanced around the office. Waggling his cigar at my diplomas and certificates on the walls, he leered, "What did it cost to bribe 'em to give you all those?"

Before sitting down, he examined his chair carefully, as if it were the electric chair in Sing Sing. After he was sworn in and it was explained that he was in effect testifying and that his words would go into the record, Groucho tried to be serious. It wasn't his strong suit, and there were many moments when he just couldn't help being the comedian. When I asked if he had any real complaints against Mrs. Marx, he replied acidly, "Intellectual incompatibility."

"Can you enlighten me on that?"

"No."

I asked if she hadn't taken courses of study at various times during the marriage in attempts to improve her mind.

"Yes," he replied. "French."

"And was she able to speak French?"

"Well, she didn't speak like De Gaulle."

"Yes, but could she carry on a conversation in French?"

"Not with me." He arched his bushy eyebrows. "I can't speak French."

Groucho had accused Eden of habitual intemperance, a charge she indignantly denied. Attempts to interrogate him on the subject brought out some of his most Marxian responses.

"In pinpointing these complaints, sir," I said, "you indicated there were empty bottles in the morning. From what you observed of the number of people in the house, you assumed that Mrs. Marx consumed those bottles?"

"Well, it wasn't the gardener.... She always had a shot in the bathroom while washing or showering."

"Did you see her drink in the bathroom?"

"Well, she didn't bathe with it."

"If you please, sir, Mrs. Marx denies she drank this much liquor, and it's my duty to find out just what you saw. You've testified you saw a bottle there, and you assumed she nipped from that bottle. But did you ever actually see her drinking in the bedroom or bathroom?"

The eyebrows went up, and he leered over his cigar. "I've seen her do *everything* in the bathroom."

Questions about his business dealings and properties elicited more hilarious testimony. Once, when his attorney interrupted Groucho's rapid-fire flow of words to remind him there wasn't any question, Groucho snapped, "I know, I know. But I like to talk."

I remember particularly his remarks when I asked about his investment in a place called Horseshoe Lake.

"It's a piece of property in either North or South Carolina where we were going to raise peaches and apples in two different states," he quipped. "One had peaches and one had apples, but the state that had the peaches got a hurricane and blew all the peaches to Pennsylvania. It just wasn't feasible to pick those peaches from South Carolina that wound up in a coal mine in Pennsylvania, so we didn't make any money on that investment."

At this point in the deposition, Groucho looked up. "You know, I thought you were a real son of a bitch when you served those papers on me. But you're not a bad guy.... What are you doing for dinner tonight?"

As the trial date approached, I stressed to Groucho's attorney that I would like to settle the case on any basis that would be fair to Eden. I reminded him that she was almost forty and, from the standpoint of her career, had given literally the best years of her life for the satisfaction of Groucho's whims. And I pointed out that rather early in the game he had forced her to choose between their marriage or her initial attempts at launching an acting career.

As the December 4 trial date approached, Eden began to develop what I call the "divorce rejection syndrome." It's a rather common malady—especially among my female clients who are married to celebrities. It begins when a woman first comes to a divorce lawyer, hurt, angry, and bitter. At that point she wants to make her husband pay—and pay dearly—for whatever he has done to drive her from his bed and board. Nothing short of unconditional surrender will suffice. But as time goes on, the hurt eases, and she is more willing to accept a negotiated peace to be "civilized" and ask nothing more than "just what is fair." And sometimes, as the actual trial date approaches, she begins to think, "Sometimes I wish I'd never started this."

With a man the feelings are more or less the same, except in the beginning he says, "Cut the bitch off without a cent." Later he admits she might be entitled to "enough to get back on her feet," and in the end he is thinking about ways to give her "one more chance" without his losing too much face.

Eden's malady wasn't as serious as most. She just became a bit overconcerned about going into court and saying things that might hurt Groucho. She felt he could never admit he was impossible to live with and would think she left him because of his age. I assured her there was little likelihood the case would go to trial because I was confident we could work out a settlement. And we did—just one day before the trial. It was an equitable settlement. Eden got $210,000 in alimony, payable over a seven-year period; more than $300,000 as her share of Groucho's television earnings, securities, and other properties; plus a home in Palm Springs, and half the value of their Grecian-style home in Trousdale Estates.

The two-minute divorce hearing was an anticlimactic event in which Eden established "mental cruelty" by stating that Groucho belittled her cooking abilities in front of his family and threatened to trade her for "a new cook and wife."

We had a much bigger trial fighting over the value of the Trousdale house. Groucho had had it appraised at a rather modest figure, but I set out to prove that its value in that movie-star-conscious community was also dependent upon who the neighbors were. I argued that the very fact that Groucho lived in it increased its value, and I spent almost three court days introducing evidence to establish the market value of neighboring residences owned by Elvis Presley, Nancy Sinatra, and Janet Leigh. In the end, the court added our figure to Groucho's figure, and split the sum down the middle.

I thought the settlement worked out fairly for both sides, but apparently Groucho did not. He let me know about it sometime later at Chasen's, the very place Eden had finally decided to end the marriage.

I was having dinner with some friends, and he noticed me as he was leaving. Stepping over to my table, he tossed his dinner check at me and said, "How about you picking up this bill, since you certainly picked me clean in my divorce?"

Before I could answer, his cigar swept an arc, and he said, "If any of these ladies at this table ever come to you, Mitchelson, don't forget who sent them!" and he stalked away. Happily, not one of them has.

CHAPTER SEVEN

The Rights of Women

I am often identified as a "woman's lawyer," and it is true that I have represented more women than men. Once on a television talk show I was asked why.

"Because," I quipped, "women have most of the money."

Later, my mother, who had watched the program, said I shouldn't say things like that in public, even if they were true. I told her the real reason was that I liked women but that I couldn't say that in public either. Actually, there's another good reason I choose to represent women—they need the protection of lawyers more. For when one looks closely at the laws of marriage and divorce, it is apparent that most of them are really strongly biased against women.

This isn't very surprising, since men have held a virtual monopoly on all positions of power down through the ages. Not until very recently has there been any equality before the law, and that happened in the United States only after the suffragette movement brought women the right to vote. But for hundreds of years the main difference between a wife and a slave was the fact that the issue of the wife's body was born free—provided it was male. In both marriage and divorce, a man was considered the lord and

MADE IN HEAVEN, SETTLED IN COURT

master of his household. His wife, and everything she possessed, became his with the marriage.

Even after the Church assumed full control of the marriage institution early in the Christian era, the economics of possession continued to be a major factor in prescribing the rules. The Church's viewpoint prevailed on monogamy as an "irrevocable" contract "made in heaven" by no less an authority than God, exercised through the good offices of His established Church, of course. But then with civil marriages no longer recognized, there was the problem of what to do about the rich and powerful who, in the Middle Ages, were no more willing to live with a bad marriage than they are today.

An Italian monk named Gratian simplified the problem in the twelfth century with a decree that provided for *divortium a vinculo* (separation from the bonds) and *divortium a mensa et thoro* (divorce from bed and board). The former was actually an annulment and could be granted only for circumstances predating the marriage (such as fraud or prior marriage), lack of consummation in the marriage, incest, and consanguinity. The latter was a legal separation in which neither party had the right to remarry. It was granted only for adultery, cruelty, and "spiritual adultery." "Spiritual adultery" meant the Church considered one of the parties a heretic or an apostate, to whom no Christian could be married without penalty of excommunication. But it wasn't grounds for *divortium a vinculo,* so the person who discovered himself married to one of these damned souls was duty-bound to seek a separation but was not free to marry again. The principles of these medieval rules survived until the reforms of the past few decades.

The slow secularization of Western divorce laws began when the Pope refused to annul the marriage of King Henry VIII of England to Catherine of Aragon. Henry's action, which split the Christian world, didn't question the Church's right to control marriage and divorce as much as it questioned the Pope's exclusive jurisdiction. The breach with Rome came when the King's Archbishop of Canterbury ruled that any ecclesiastical court had the power to grant a divorce. From that time on, Englishmen, like English kings, could divorce their wives if Parliament sanctioned the convening of a religious court to hear the issue.

The secularization was extended still more when early Protestant reformers, including the Puritans, demanded that divorce laws be eased and Church control ended. The poet John Milton made a fervent plea for reform when he stated that grounds for a divorce should be "indisposition, unfitness, or contrariety of mind, arising from a cause in nature unchangeable, hindering and ever likely to hinder, the main benefits of conjugal society, which are solace in peace." Or—in a word—incompatibility.

Milton maintained that all who sought divorces should be granted them because "it is less a breach of wedlock to part with wise and quiet consent betimes, than still to soil and profane that mystery of joy and union with a polluting sadness and a perpetual distemper. . . ." No better argument has been advanced by proponents of relaxed divorce laws in the more than 300 years that have since passed.

When the American colonies were settled, Puritans and Quakers who had fought for divorce law reforms in England tried to introduce them in America. In some instances, they succeeded, and brought down the wrath of both Crown and Parliament, who declared that all such laws in the colonies were annulled. At stake were the traditional fees paid to the Crown and the bribes paid to key members of Parliament. Previously, if a colonist wanted a divorce, it had to be granted through proper parliamentary procedure, and neither the King nor his ministers were willing to give up the resultant revenues. Among the final list of grievances that led to the American Revolution was the Crown's and Parliament's ruling that the colonists were not permitted to establish their own divorce laws.

With the coming of American independence, the church officially dropped out of the marriage and divorce picture since our Constitution specifically separated church and state. But what is law isn't necessarily fact, and there developed the anomaly of religious marriage being granted automatic civil validity while religious divorce has no force in law at all. The Constitution also gave the power of making divorce laws to the various states, creating a jurisdictional muddle that has yet to be resolved. But most states were quick to follow the lead of their English forebears, and the right to grant a divorce was almost universally reserved for the legislatures.

But the trend toward judicial divorce did not hold much sway until the Civil War, and then it did only because American legislators tended to sell divorces as much as grant them, creating an open scandal. The new judicial divorce laws required that "guilt" be established before a divorce could be granted, which turned the process into an adversary proceeding much like a criminal trial. The states that allowed divorce (for a century South Carolina even refused to grant it) made adultery the prime ground. Many also added cruelty, desertion, and conviction of a felonious crime.

The opening of the West provided impetus for the easing of divorce laws in new states which sought to attract settlers. In time Ohio, Illinois, and Indiana became such divorce meccas that one Indiana editor lamented: "We are overrun by a flock of ill-used and ill-using, petulant, libidinous, extravagant, ill-fitting husbands and wives, as a sink is overrun with the foul water of a whole house."

The easy divorce laws primarily benefited men seeking to shed responsibilities who wanted to pack up and run, leaving wives, children, and old failures behind. The exodus of such men from the East helped make divorce laws one of the targets of the first organized battle for women's rights.

Elizabeth Cady Stanton, one of the earliest and most vociferous champions of her sex, expressed her outrage at the state of things by publicly charging:

The male has spoken in Scripture. He has spoken in law. As an individual, he has decided the time and cause for putting away a wife, and as judge and legislator, he still holds the entire control.

Her charge was answered editorially by the supposedly liberal newspaper publisher, the great Horace Greeley, who harangued:

To the libertine, the egotist, the selfish, sensual seeker of personal and present enjoyment at whatever cost to others, the Indissolubility of Marriage is an obstacle, a restraint, a terror; God forbid it should ever cease to be.

("Let us hope," Mrs. Stanton rejoined, "that all wisdom does not live, and will not die, with Horace Greeley.")

But the real fight was more with organized religious groups, who held sway over state legislatures, and women still lacked the right to vote. Gradually, in the name of fairness, women were granted some concessions within the established system, and laws were passed giving them the right to sue for breach of promise and alienation of affections.

To protect the sanctity that the law stated was due the home and marriage, most states passed strict criminal statutes against adultery and fornication, with many statutes codifying the acts loosely under amorphous terms such as "illicit relations" and, in California, "resorting." The idea was to make jail the penalty for all nonmarital sexual acts.

Certain notorious New York lawyers used the divorce, breach of promise, and alienation of affections laws as personal keys to the mint. Politically powerful and completely devoid of ethics, such lawyers did much to give the legal practice of domestic relations a bad name, yet at the same time they unwittingly helped keep the spirit of divorce reform alive. Leaders in the women's rights struggle, such as Frances Willard and Carrie Chapman Catt, lobbied and petitioned for divorce law reform. Though it never ranked as high in their priorities as suffrage did (or national Prohibition), it remained one of the major planks in their platform.

A great many social inequities have been corrected and legal barriers toppled since women won their right to vote. But after almost two decades of legal practice, I still find the law is weighted against them in many ways.

And despite some of the most sweeping legal and social changes in history, there is little difference among the women clients who consult with me. In the main, they seem to fall into three types. The first may be characterized as the "angry wife." Though she frequently comes into my office wanting to sue everybody in sight—her husband, his alleged girl friend or girl friends, his business partners, the bank, and no telling who else—she can be reasoned with. In fact, once she calms down and understands that it is not the function of the law to punish her husband, she often becomes one of those most likely to succumb to the "divorce rejection syndrome"—i.e., second thoughts.

The other two types are opposite sides of the same coin but might be called the "reluctant clients." One is the woman who doesn't want a divorce but is actually forced, or feels she is forced, into it. The other is the woman who really wants a divorce, but for one reason or another is afraid of the consequences and the uncertain future, a situation quite common in long-term marriages that have gone stale.

Singer Connie Stevens' divorce from Eddie Fisher falls in the class of a genuinely forced divorce. I first met her at one of actor Richard Harris's parties, shortly after she and Eddie were married. Richard reminded Connie, who was just recently divorced from Jim Stacy, that if she ever needed another divorce lawyer, I specialized in the field. She replied that another divorce lawyer was the last person she would ever need. But two years later I was on a night flight to Las Vegas at the request of her business manager, who told me Connie was having some marital problems and needed to meet with me.

Connie is the gentlest woman I have ever met. Though she was terribly upset and depressed when I talked with her that night in her dressing room at the Flamingo, it did not diminish her basic warmth. She didn't want a divorce or a divorce lawyer, even then. But she needed one, for Eddie had told her that he didn't want to be married any more.

Connie couldn't understand it and was still so much in love she couldn't accept it. Her whole world was wrapped up in her husband and their two infant daughters. I had watched her show before our meeting and had marveled at her standing there during the finale still able to sing songs dedicated to Eddie and the girls, while giant pictures of them flashed on a screen behind her. That *is* show biz.

"There's no reason for a divorce," she pleaded. "Please talk to Eddie and his lawyers."

The lawyers assured me Eddie was prepared to file the suit if Connie didn't. When I called to tell her of the planned suit and urge that she act first, she insisted Eddie would never do anything like that. But he did—the very next day.

Connie had made it plain she wanted no financial settlement, though under California law at that time, "guilt" was still a factor in divorce proceedings. Neither would she let me fight for her, even though Eddie hadn't bothered to call and tell her he was filing. She found out secondhand after the news media had published the word.

Connie was a lady who really didn't want anything; it was her brother and business manager who were the ones who urged me to protect her interests. I had trouble even getting her to accept the idea of child support. She was a "stand on your own two feet" kind of person, with the liberated view that no woman should take anything from anybody if she could make it by herself.

Still, Connie thought Eddie would never actually go through with the divorce. It took a final—and unnecessary—act of cruelty to make her accept the facts. She was on tour with the children in New York when she found out that Eddie had packed up all of the children's toys and belongings in an attempt to have them removed from the family home. I immediately got a restraining order that prohibited Eddie from removing any of the children's things.

But when the divorce was granted, Connie not only refused to ask for alimony, but was unwilling to even accept her share of the community property. In fact, it was only after much argument that she reluctantly agreed to accept rather modest child-support payments from Eddie. She was a client who was truly forced into a divorce. And I don't believe she really accepted it as final and over until the moment the judge said, "Decree granted."

A good example of a woman who felt she was forced to seek a divorce is probably Joanna Ray, a pretty, charming English girl whose father was surgeon to the Queen. Her problems seemed to stem mainly from a sweet disposition, a reserved demeanor, and a husband who drank. She was, like Connie, just so nice you really couldn't help her. At the time Joanna reluctantly came to me seeking to end her marriage, her husband, actor Aldo Ray, had acquired a lot of property and made some very good investments. But his off-stage behavior had become so erratic that the studios wouldn't hire him, and he was beginning to make some bad business decisions. Naturally, such circumstances only served to increase Ray's sullen and sometimes violent behavior, making it impossible for Joanna and their two children to live with him.

I always had to pry information from her, to pick and probe as if I were cross-examining a hostile witness, even at the initial interview. After the divorce—which Ray took rather hard, since he was very fond of his children—things didn't get much better because Joanna still didn't want to hurt him, and I had to almost force her to protect herself. She got a fair settlement, but Ray tended to fall behind in his support payments. She never told me about it, though, until he was anywhere from ten months to two years behind with them. As a result, I was never able to do as much for her as I would have liked. She was reluctant to take him to court and always forgave him whenever he made an effort to catch up.

The third type of woman who comes to me is typified by the almost classic case of one who wants a divorce but is afraid to seek it until many years after the marriage should have ended. Her case also typifies the kind of marriage that dies because the couple has simply drifted apart during the years. She begins to feel trapped and begins thinking about a divorce but doesn't have the courage to initiate it.

Many women, especially in long marital situations, have this problem. They know the relationship is finished, but they just keep hanging in there without really knowing why. Sometimes it's fear of the unknown, of what it might be like being on their own. They put it off with the rationalization that "Well, at least I have security," or "My husband has a name and is respected and I'm still Mrs. . . ." In cases like this, it is important to act decisively. It puts the husband off balance and lessens the chance that he or his lawyers can pressure the wife back into a marriage she no longer wants. Decisive action such as tying up the couple's assets with pretrial restraining orders may be important, since women are often not knowledgeable about family business affairs, and quick action may be needed to keep the parties' assets intact. The most important effect of decisive action, however, is the indirect psychological boost it gives the woman, for it lets the husband know that the wife he has dominated so completely for so long is finally ready to stand up for her rights and has an attorney willing to protect those rights.

CHAPTER EIGHT

Dividing a Dream House

Rhonda Fleming came to me after the 1970 Family Law "no-fault" divorce law went into effect in California. Prior to that law, there were five grounds for divorce in California, the most common one being mental cruelty. Others were habitual intemperance, desertion, adultery, and incurable insanity. To get a divorce, one spouse had to prove the other guilty of one of these offenses. If one party charged mental cruelty and the other party contested and cross-filed on the same charge, and if both charges were proven, the judge would grant each party a divorce and the property would then be divided fifty-fifty. If, however, one party proved the mental cruelty charge against the other, then generally more than 50 percent was granted the "winning" side.

The new law was considered to be a model law in that it eliminated guilt by eliminating fault. Since its passage, the only ground for divorce in California (other than incurable insanity) is "irreconcilable differences." Either party may obtain a divorce simply by testifying that such differences exist. In a statutory attempt to eliminate the traditional stigma of blame associated with divorce, the proceeding is now called a "dissolution" and the marriage is said to be "dissolved."

The new law had another aim: it sought to eliminate disputes over division of property by requiring that community property be divided equally between the parties. But legislation is not always effective where money is concerned, and there is always a battle—sometimes a battle royal—over who gets what.

Despite the progressiveness of the new no-fault law in California, the Rhonda Fleming-Hall Bartlett divorce was tried with all the heat and passion the new law was supposed to eliminate. It proved to me that no matter how liberal a law may be, when people part who have loved very much and have had a relationship of the deepest nature, the act of divorce makes a harsh catharsis indeed.

If any marriage could possibly have been said to work, certainly the Fleming-Bartlett marriage should have—even in California, where 60 percent of the population experiences at least one divorce. The case convinced me Pamela Mason was right when she titled her book *Marriage Is the First Step Toward Divorce.* As the statuesque, flame-haired film discovery of David O. Selznick, Rhonda had starred in many motion pictures, and when she and Hall were married she was still active in television, summer stock, and Las Vegas productions. Hall was a versatile film producer, screenwriter, and director whose productions included *Sandpit Generals* (which was a winner at the Moscow Film Festival) and later, *Jonathan Livingston Seagull.* The pair had similar and complementary backgrounds and shared a great many interests outside of their profession.

Both were in their forties at the time of their marriage and had been through prior unsuccessful attempts. They obviously had experience enough to avoid the usual pitfalls that plague the very young. Certainly they knew enough not to romanticize the institution as a never-ending soiree of ecstatic happiness. With the past to learn from, they had a good idea of what they wanted and an equally good idea of what could be expected.

Very early in the relationship, Hall was critically injured in an explosion when a hot water heater blew up. Rhonda's attention during his long months of recovery was a tribute to the strength of her devotion and contributed much to their subsequent determination to make the marriage work. Indeed they did work hard to make a go of it, planning life together as they planned the dream home which was to stand as a monument to the perfect marriage.

The home, on Stone Canyon Road in Bel-Air, was built of the best materials available, and its construction far exceeded the usual building and safety code standards of the day. They intended it to last forever, just as they intended their marriage to last. They furnished the house with beautiful furniture and fine art, and when the project was finished they sought to immortalize it in a privately printed, beautifully bound book entitled *The Bartletts Build Their Dream House.*

When the marriage died, they fought more bitterly over that house and its furnishings than over anything else.

In trying to analyze what went wrong with what should have been a perfect marriage, I can only conclude that perhaps they tried too hard to live out their storybook romance in a manner usually reserved for beginners. There was also the drawback that by middle age people's habits and attitudes are usually fairly well set. Little compromises are always necessary, of course, when two people try to live as one, no matter how similar their interests or backgrounds; but when the flexibility to adjust to things easily is missing, ego often gets in the way of these compromises. The Bartletts wanted to adjust to each other in order to build a new life together, but when it came down to specifics it just didn't work out that way. Rhonda and Hall were very strong-willed people, and both had become accustomed to having things pretty much their own way. Since show business people spend so much of the time "on stage" where their images as personalities are always at stake, they are particularly prone to treat all conflicts or disagreements as ego threats. So disagreements became threats to the Bartletts' individual personalities rather than mere differences of opinion.

The couple's past may also have worked against them—at least psychologically. With three prior marriages each and having done very little of the usual personal adjusting necessary, they entered the fourth with perhaps a loser's philosophy in the marital arts. In their case, experience told them the world wouldn't end if their marriage failed. Like most temptations, divorce is most difficult the first time; after that, it becomes progressively easier. Thus, the psychological impact of these experiences would make almost anyone willing to give up—and willing to give up quicker.

The Fleming-Bartlett divorce case had about every conceivable problem possible, not the least of which was that neither lawyer had very good control of his client. This, plus a judge determined to move the case along (it was now in its second year), turned it into a full-blown trial.

Rhonda knew her own mind, had a pretty good idea of her rights, and was willing to battle anyone to protect them—including her own attorney. The disagreement came over what she considered those rights to be. It was what caused the dismissal of her original lawyer and brought her to me. It isn't unusual for clients— quite often without any real reason—to switch lawyers during a case. This is especially true in the domestic relations field where some clients change attorneys as frequently as they do spouses. Sometimes there are sound reasons for it, as when the initial attorney is a family or business lawyer who does not specialize in domestic relations and who may himself recommend the change. In other instances, a client and attorney may discover their temperaments clash too greatly and the desire for change becomes mutual, since no lawyer really wants to battle his own client.

I found Rhonda could be led by logic, but couldn't be pushed. Fortunately, we never had a serious disagreement, though I learned there were areas where my logic wouldn't work. One of them, of course, was the Bartlett Dream Home and its contents. Hall was as adamant as Rhonda on that subject and both of them fought bitterly against any compromise.

Before I came into the case, they had tried to work out an arrangement for them both to continue living in the house during the divorce proceedings. The mere issuance of restraining orders is often not enough, in which parties are commanded not to harm, molest, harass, or annoy one another, and yet are put in separate wings of the same house. That is a difficult situation, even under the best of circumstances. Here it was next to impossible. It had been the dream home of a dream marriage, and though the marriage dream had faded, the house was very real, and both of them wanted it badly. Since it was a large house, populated only by the Bartletts themselves, it might have been argued it was big enough for both to live in separately without running into each other very often—provided the emotional aspects were ignored. But from my experience I have found that when two people are in the middle of a bitter divorce, even a twenty-two room mansion isn't big enough to house both of them, if for no other reason than that there is only one front door for both of them to walk through—the second party is not going to agree to leave by way of the side or back door. It's sometimes possible to have the court exclude one party from the home pending trial of the divorce, if you can make a strong enough showing that it's dangerous to your client's health or safety to have the other person on the premises. But it has to be a really dangerous—usually physically harmful—situation. While it's possible to argue that the other spouse's presence is psychologically dangerous to the client's health, the courts seldom order anyone out of the house for this reason alone.

Prior attorneys for Rhonda and Hall had worked out an agreement for living in the Dream House according to a rather complex formula which became even more complex and finally required court intervention. Later, in fact, we were compelled to apply to the court several times to ask the judge to settle the housing disputes.

Initially, the Bartletts had taken separate wings of the house and set up timetables for use of the kitchen and pool. The agreement prohibited Rhonda from having male visitors and Hall from having female guests. All necessary communications between the two were transmitted with written notes delivered by the maid. Then the maid, who had been with the Bartletts for many years, became a problem. Rhonda complained that she spied on her and listened to her telephone calls, and she demanded a maid of her own as well as a separate telephone. Bartlett then hired a second maid for himself, and Rhonda complained his two maids ganged up on her maid. Finally, a judge ordered the third maid out. We also had to get a court order excluding all relatives from the home because Rhonda complained about Hall's teenaged daughters staying there, and he complained about her sister's lengthy visits.

But the problems of maintaining a truce in the Dream House-turned-battleground were minor compared to the problems of dividing community property—or, more accurately, deciding whether or not there was any community property to divide. Bartlett said there wasn't, that he'd made no money during the marriage, and that everything (including the home) was his own separate property. His claim was strengthened because, as a result of the accident before their marriage, he hadn't been able to produce pictures during the first few years of his recovery. When he finally did start again, the pictures he produced didn't show any profit, and one (called *Changes*) lost money. The money for the pictures—and for the house—had either come from Hall's father's estate or had been gifts from his mother. We argued that even though the money to produce the films came from his mother, the film properties were produced during the marriage and were, therefore, community property. Not all of the pictures were failures and at the time of the trial *Sandpit Generals,* we felt, had a very high box-office potential.

We also pointed out that the deed to the house was in both their names and contended that even if the property had been separate originally, by now their assets were co-mingled and Bartlett had agreed to share them by "oral transmutation" before the marriage. An oral transmutation is in effect an unwritten transfer of property from one person to another.

When the trial started, my task was to convince the court that this oral transmutation (Bartlett's promise to share his assets with Rhonda) had actually taken place. Although Bartlett denied it, we contended that he had persuaded Rhonda to give up a profitable acting career on the promise that he would share his fortune with her. To back up this contention, we were planning to introduce some of his early love letters to Rhonda and the testimony of movie columnist Dorothy Manners.

Both sides tried to work out a settlement right up to the time the trial started. The trial itself lasted two weeks. I called Miss Manners, an internationally recognized authority on the entertainment world, as my first witness to prove that Bartlett had asked Rhonda to give up her career and that he publicly stated the Dream House was something the two of them had built together and always intended to share.

The columnist was an excellent witness who came well prepared to testify, bringing interview notes to back up her statements. She had interviewed Bartlett both before the marriage and while the house was under construction. When she was on the witness stand, I read from the published interview that quoted Bartlett as saying he wanted Rhonda to quit working after they married and asked her what he had said. She was able to verify from her notes that the exact words were: "I want her to stop working." Asked about Bartlett's comments in the Dream House interview, she said his exact words were: "This is something we're doing together. It's going to be our home. Something we'll always share." Later Miss Manners testified that it would be possible for Rhonda to resume her career, but not easy. "You can't come back after five or six years; it's certain death in the entertainment industry," she said. "It will be almost like starting again for her. It would be for anyone."

We introduced *The Bartletts Build Their Dream House* into evidence, and when Rhonda took the stand I asked her if Bartlett had ever called the house his separate property. "No," she replied. "He always referred to it as 'ours.' That was the whole point of the book." In regard to his making references to other separate property or money, she testified: "No, never at any time. After all, we were married and we shared everything. He told me that was what we'd do before we were married." About her carreer she testified: "He told me he didn't want me to continue working, that there wasn't any need after we married because we'd share everything."

To back up her testimony, I introduced his love letters and read extensively from them in my cross-examination of Bartlett. They were quite eloquent—the judge even commented that Bartlett had a nice style. They were also quite damaging. Bartlett predictably insisted that his comments about stopping Rhonda's career and sharing his fortune were misinterpreted. He said he only meant by them that she should stop doing road shows because they took her away from home and that he had only meant that his wealth would be shared while they were married—not given to her. He freely admitted that the house deed was in both names and that he always referred to it as "our home." But, he insisted that since he had paid for it, the house belonged to him alone.

His attorney then sought to introduce some writings in

Rhonda's hand which, he claimed, showed a plan, or "blueprint," for divorcing Bartlett and "getting as much money as possible." He inferred it was some kind of plot conceived by Rhonda and her sister. However, the "blueprint" turned out to be some notes Rhonda had taken down during a consultation with the renowned English clairvoyant, Maurice Woodward, who had predicted the divorce and many of the subsequent events, including, even, that Bartlett would buy Rhonda a blue car, which he did.

Late Friday of the second week the judge, in no uncertain terms, told us we were going to have to complete the case even if we had to stay in the courtroom all night. It didn't take that long, but it was well into the night before we were finished.

The final award to Rhonda seemed fair, though not what she had hoped to get. She had really wanted the Dream House, but while the judge did declare it was part of the community property, he awarded it to Bartlett on condition that he buy Rhonda's share, otherwise the house was to be sold and the profits divided. He also ordered them to divide up the dream house's furnishings and warned if they couldn't reach an agreement he would appoint a referee to act as an agent of the court with power to arbitrate any disputes and make binding decisions on who got what.

The bitterness and the enmity that characterized virtually every step of the Bartlett divorce proceedings continued into the division of the furniture, and the referee (yes, they finally had to have one) had to work "all fifteen rounds" before a decision could be reached as to who would get what furniture. It shows rather clearly, I think, that even the best legislation is incapable of removing guilt or fault from the minds of people who cling to the idea that marriage should work and then find out it doesn't. Apparently, neither Hall nor Rhonda could accept the idea that perhaps the fault lies with the institution itself and not necessarily with the persons involved, although others may disagree. Despite the California lawmakers' removal of all traces of fault from the 1970 Family Law, the rising divorce rate in our country proves that people have not lost *their* ability to find fault with each other.

CHAPTER NINE

For Richer or for Poorer

There are three issues common to every divorce, and all involve money. They are support for the children, alimony for the wife, and division of the property between the two parties. Once love flies out the window, the transition from passion to purse is frequently instantaneous.

Virtually every state recognizes the father's responsibility to support his children. In fact, many states today have reciprocal agreements with other states for enforcing child-support orders. These agreements allow legal authorities of one state to bring the delinquent father into court to collect money owed children who reside in another state.

However, no provision was made for a divorced wife to receive alimony (spousal support, as it is now called in California) until the 1870s. She had to find some other way to support herself, be supported by her family, or find a new man to take care of her. New York, Pennsylvania, and Ohio were the first states to pass laws granting alimony, but within a few years every state had made some such provision. The women's rights organizations lobbied strongly for these laws (along with others intended to protect women from exploitation), but probably greater pressure was exerted by the increased number of women who were becoming public charges, supported at the taxpayers' expense.

The legal concept that women are entitled to alimony or property settlements is a relatively new one. Less than a hundred years ago it was still generally recognized that all property belonged to the man. Some states retained laws that forbade women to own property. The concept of community property—the idea that assets acquired during a marriage are jointly owned—came from Spain, and for a long time only those states once ruled by Spain (such as California and Texas) made any provision for community property rights in their laws.

Many states that currently do not have community property laws recognize that women are entitled to some of the property accumulated during a marriage. In states that do not have "no-fault" divorce laws, the "guilt" or degree of misconduct of either party is frequently considered with as much diligence as is the amount of a wife's financial contribution during the marriage.

As a former Spanish possession, California has always been a community property state. But before the no-fault dissolution of marriage law was passed in 1970, judges had considerable leeway in dividing the community property. They could award less, more, or all of the assets to either party—based on the "guilt" of one person or the other.

Property settlements were always difficult under the old law, but often they are no easier under the new one. The battle now, however, is not over division of the property but over its definition. The one who has possession says "It's mine." The other insists "It's ours." One lawyer's idea of equality is frequently another's definition of robbery.

There are many ways of defining what is, and isn't, community property. Generally speaking, property (whether real or intangible), that is owned by either party before the marriage remains his or her separate property, unless it is subsequently co-mingled, or mixed in, with the community assets. All assets earned or acquired after the marriage (unless by gift or inheritance) are considered part of the community finances. Of course the divorcing spouses or their attorneys frequently differ on how "earned," "acquired," or "co-mingled" should be defined— especially when disputed property is involved.

For a long time the law held that real property standing in a married woman's name alone was presumed to be separate property, while similar property in a man's name was presumed community property. It was one of the few instances where the law apparently worked to a man's detriment. There are also prenuptial agreements that have varying amounts of validity in determining the extent of community assets. The law remains extremely flexible on these issues, and when attorneys can reach no agreement, the court makes the decision, often not to the complete satisfaction of either party.

I once had a client whose husband claimed that their $600,000 home was his separate property, though he had given her a solid gold key inscribed, *To my darling wife, my gift to you,* and though we were able to produce more than a dozen witnesses who testified he had repeatedly stated in public that the house was jointly owned. I considered we had ample proof of an "oral transmutation," one of the special ways separate property can be turned into community property.

Although he argued that the house was built with his own money, the husband's only witness was the loan officer of his bank, and the only document offered into evidence was the deed, which stood in his name alone. The loan officer testified that he considered the deed sufficient proof of sole ownership and that he had accepted it as collateral for a loan. I didn't feel that the considerations of the deed had any relevance to our claim. But the judge ruled the house was separate property, and the appellate courts upheld the ruling.

I have discovered over the years that wives frequently have little concept of community property laws and less of family assets, either in terms of what these are or where they might be found. Consequently, financial experts, who seem to be half bookkeeper and half bloodhound, have largely replaced the old-time private eyes who spent so much time trying to ferret out romantic trysts. Many wives are happily amazed to learn the extent of the community property after it has been brought to light; others are shocked by the degree of its concealment.

Some men are very open and aboveboard in listing their assets. Others go to such extremes to conceal their wealth that the Mafia could probably take lessons. Even the best-hidden assets can usually be found, however, by the liberal use of financial investigators and what is known as the discovery process, which is a pretrial legal process that gives an attorney the right to go on almost any kind of hunting expedition for information and allows him to use a shotgun approach while doing it.

In discovery proceedings almost nothing is considered irrelevant or immaterial. It isn't necessary to lay a foundation for any question. Hearsay, which is barred from the courtroom, may be used as the basis for both subpoenaing information and questioning the witness. If the potential witness refuses to answer questions, a court order can be obtained to make him do so. All answers are given under oath, and if the witness lies he is subject to the penalty of perjury. All personal financial records, corporate records, and income-tax returns can be demanded, and court orders can be obtained to open (sometimes to seal) safe-deposit boxes.

Sometimes in the discovery process, the smallest inconsistencies can lead to major recoveries. I once took the deposition of the husband of a woman I was representing who was so open and forthright I was almost certain he was hiding nothing. But in checking his records, we noticed he had deducted $32 for safe-deposit boxes. He had told us about a safe-deposit box, but a call to his bank revealed that the standard charge was only $8 per box.

We set another deposition hearing. During the questioning, I told him, "I know it was an oversight, but when you told us about the Bank of America safe-deposit box you neglected to mention the locations of the others."

Phrasing it that way provided an opening that still allowed him to keep his self-respect. He had no way of knowing how we had learned about the other boxes, but he realized we had, and he made no further effort at concealing them. The additional boxes revealed stacks of securities worth hundreds of thousands of dollars, which made quite a difference in the final financial settlement.

An attorney has to be rather hard-nosed and thorough in these pretrial discovery proceedings—not only to protect his client but also to protect himself. Any slipshod, careless work during discovery may lead to the possibility of being sued for malpractice or disciplined by the bar. By law the attorney has a fiduciary responsibility to the client, and professional standards require that he exercise all "due diligence" in carrying out this responsibility—in short, he is expected to peer under every rock and into every crevice.

I once had a client whose husband owned a large manufacturing firm. In the course of discovery proceedings we unearthed an almost perfect scheme for concealing community assets.

The books showed that the company had a branch factory in Monterrey, Mexico, which over a period of years had lost more than $450,000. The records were complete, but I sent a financial investigator down there anyway to see if there was some way to salvage any money out of the branch for my client. The investigator called a few hours after arriving to ask if I was certain it was Monterrey, Mexico, and not Monterey, California, since he couldn't find the factory or any indication that it ever existed. A subsequent check of Mexican records proved that the plant was a total myth.

Later, when I was taking the husband's deposition, I brought up the subject of the Mexican plant. "Is it in Monterrey, *Mexico?*"

He gave me a rather guarded look. "That's right, Mexico."

I told him before we went any further that, since we had sent an investigator to Mexico, he ought to consult with his attorney.

His lawyer gave me a puzzled look. "What's to discuss? He's given you all the facts."

"Why don't you go into my conference room anyway," I replied. "I am sure he has something to tell you."

When they returned a few moments later, his attorney was red-faced and grim. The manufacturer, however, wasn't even contrite. "It cost me $5,000 to set up those books," he said. "And I think it ought to come out of the community property."

After all the property involved in a marriage is discovered and identified as community or separate, the question still remains of how it should be divided. Because this is an age of high taxation and sophisticated tax loopholes, the method of division frequently becomes the most lengthy and complicated issue in negotiating a financial settlement. Most divorce lawyers find they must rely heavily on tax experts at this stage of the proceedings.

Alimony is tax deductible for the party who pays it. Child-support payments are not deductible. A parent has a legal obligation to support his child and receives no tax benefit regardless of whether or not he has custody. On the other hand, the parent receiving financial support incurs no tax liability from child-care payments; however, alimony is considered taxable income. Therefore, if the children are young or the alimony is restricted in duration, it's usually to the wife's advantage to have the child-support payments set high and the alimony set relatively low. Conversely, it's to the husband's advantage to set the alimony high and the child support low—especially if the court follows the current trend of limiting the duration of alimony or spousal support.

There was a time when most alimony was awarded "until death or remarriage," particularly if there was a lengthy marriage. But with present opportunities for women to find employment, judges more and more tend to limit support to a period considered reasonably necessary to find work or complete work training.

The primary concern of tax consultants and financial experts who are called to give aid in financial settlements is to help the attorney get the maximum benefit for his client. The biggest assets do not always yield the greatest monetary returns. One asset may be subject to later capital gains taxes, while another is not. One can show promise of appreciating in value over a period of years, while another shows signs of becoming worthless in time. It might be mutually advantageous to split the property on a less than fifty-fifty basis in return for higher or longer alimony and child-support payments. Sometimes the husband's career and business potential, even his health, make lump-sum cash or property settlements more advantageous than the most liberal and long-term support agreements.

Division of community property is of interest to the Internal Revenue Service only so far as it affects the current year's income for each party. Taxes for prior years are presumed to have been paid. But the specter of the tax man lurks in the background of every divorce where large amounts of income or income-producing property are at stake, and there have been occasions when public revelation of such property settlements caused the IRS to review past returns, sometimes with disastrous results to the parties of the divorce.

I have represented clients whose post-divorce tax problems left them nearly as destitute as the women who became public charges in the days before alimony. Two such cases involved women who were not my clients at the time of their divorces, but came to me later on related matters. Their plight was typical of many victims of the IRS's unsympathetic way of collecting taxes.

Evie Johnson had divorced her husband, Van, after a twenty-five-year marriage during which he became a very big star. She had an alimony agreement based on a percentage of his earnings which would have provided her with a fairly decent living—except for tax troubles. Van was still working regularly, though his career was beginning to decline, and he couldn't command nearly as high a salary anymore, but the IRS had placed a $250,000 lien against him for back taxes.

The taxes had been assessed after the divorce, but that meant nothing to the IRS. The government is a special kind of creditor. It doesn't wait to be paid, it simply goes in and takes, and it doesn't care who pays the money, or how much, if any, is left after the tax bite. With Evie it was always a race with the IRS for Van's check—and the IRS usually won.

The Johnsons were really victims of a common Hollywood occupational hazard. Many movie stars adopt a lifestyle that sometimes goes beyond their income even though they are at the height of their careers. Long after they can no longer afford to maintain it, they continue to live as if they could. I wasn't able to help Evie much because there was nothing to be done, for although Van was willing to pay the alimony, the IRS kept taking it over as payment against the lien. In lieu of a retainer, Evie gave me a pair of antique Chinese statues. I ended up giving them back to her because there was nothing I could possibly do with her case.

I had more luck with Mary Cummings, ex-wife of actor Bob Cummings. Her problem was a little different and, as a result, I was able to get some cooperation from the IRS.

The Cummings' tax problem arose long after their divorce when a tax shelter investment in the Bahamas was ruled invalid by the IRS, and the U.S. government demanded increased income taxes from all the previous years, plus penalties and interest. Mrs. Cummings had a divorce settlement which included the family home and a combination of property and support payments sufficient to maintain her and the children in relative comfort. Included in the terms was Cummings' agreement to hold her harmless from any tax liabilities arising out of the marriage.

Unfortunately, the Federal Government does not consider itself bound by state court or private-party agreements. When the back taxes came due, Cummings had a new position as an executive in a health foods organization which specialized in dealer participation. Since his role was essentially a promotional one, the firm furnished him with a company-owned home and a rather lavish expense account—neither of which the IRS could touch. So the government went after Mary, seized her assets, and actually sold the home out from under her. I was able to help a little bit in two ways: the IRS agreed not to go after any increases in support payments, and the court agreed to increase both alimony and child support after considering the loss of income Mrs. Cummings suffered as the result of the government divesting her of the income-providing properties.

The courts are reluctant to reopen the issue of a financial settlement where real property or cash assets are involved unless there is a case of fraud. The complaint of falling into a tax-trap pitfall is seldom considered sufficient grounds. For this reason, and because of the increased complexity of business and personal taxation, divorce lawyers will no doubt continue to find it necessary to consult with tax and financial experts. Such consultation with relatively disinterested third parties are almost always easier than dealing with the combatants themselves.

CHAPTER TEN

The Politics of Reconciliation

Richard Harris is a big, red-haired Irishman with an ebullient nature and an overwhelming manner. He is also a marvelous actor who I sometimes think can never quite stop playing Richard Harris or fully define the role he is really seeking.

A free, even anarchistic soul, he feels bound by no rules except his own—and they are constantly in flux. Though life is real to him, it's never in earnest. If whiskey weren't made to be drunk, why was it made at all? If women weren't made to . . . and so on. I met him ten years ago at one of the nonstop parties in California that made him an instant celebrity when he arrived from England and established his legendary capacity for having a good time and an ability to hold his liquor.

A few days after the party he met with me and began haranguing the English courts and his noble-born wife, Elizabeth, for subjecting him to the indignities of a divorce action. The divorce laws of England were "antediluvian!" his wife's charges against him "unimportant!" and the British jurists "all a bunch of bewigged, begowned fossils!"

When I finally was able to interrupt the extravagant performance long enough to ask why he was telling me all this, he roared, "Damn it, man! Because I want you to represent me!"

When I started to explain the necessity of having an English attorney for an English divorce, he snorted, "Who said anything about a divorce? I want you to work out a reconciliation."

Reconciliations are hardly a divorce lawyer's specialty, but most of us do try when the chances look good. Actually, there is a professional duty imposed on a lawyer to seek a reconciliation whenever possible. This, however, wasn't one of those situations. Elizabeth, daughter of Lord and Lady Ogmore, had filed the suit in London and had listed about every ground in the English law books, including intemperance, infidelity, cruelty, and desertion. Richard had countersued, using many of the same grounds. Two handsome packages of complaints.

I tried to point out the many reasons his request was impractical, including the fact that he should be the one to talk reconciliation with Elizabeth.

"But she won't talk to me," he complained.

"Well, under British law," I explained to him, "I'd have to get her solicitor's approval before I could even try to talk with her."

"That shouldn't be any problem," he persisted. "You know him. It's David Jacobs."

I did indeed. David and I had been associates in many cases involving people in the entertainment world in London and in the United States. This made Richard's request a potential conflict of interest, since lawyers in association should not represent both parties in a lawsuit.

My attempt to interpose this problem didn't faze Richard at all. "So what's unethical about a reconciliation?" he demanded. "We'll all be working to save the marriage instead of ending it, won't we? All for one and one for all, with everybody on the side of the angels."

With similarly brilliant cock-eyed logic he beat down every argument I raised. In the end I told him I would sound David out on the subject. I was relatively sure he'd reject the suggestion, and even if he didn't I thought I could still bow out of the case.

I was wrong on both counts.

Richard wouldn't let me off the hook. He kept calling between takes at the studio where they were filming, always with the same two questions: Had I talked with David Jacobs? When could I go to London to see Elizabeth? Every time he saw a newspaper or magazine story mentioning his much publicized troubles, he either read them over the phone to me or mailed me copies with messages scrawled on them as "How much longer must I suffer these outrageous slings and arrows!"

Although I wanted to help Richard, who was not then a client, I was concerned about damaging my relationship with David. I procrastinated as long as possible, until Richard was finished with his work in California and had been signed to do *Camelot* which was to be filmed in Spain. At that point I realized I had to make a decision and got on the phone to call David. To my surprise, he agreed to the proposal. Richard, of course, thought it was wonderful and urged me to go to London immediately to see Elizabeth while he went on to Spain.

When I arrived in London, I first paid a courtesy call on David, since I still felt uneasy about the situation.

"Quite frankly, Marvin," David said, "for anyone else I would have refused out of hand."

It was understandable. The divorce action was before the court. Under British law I had no standing in the case at all. My intrusion, in fact, could have an adverse effect on David's relationship with Elizabeth or on the lawsuit itself. It could even cost him an important client.

Elizabeth Harris, a petite, aristocratic blonde, was polite but skeptical of Richard's dramatic gesture of sending an American lawyer to plead his suit. She was in no mood to discuss a reconciliation with Richard under any terms. And she made it clear that she considered any further meetings would be a waste of my time and hers.

When I telephoned Richard in Spain, he paid no more attention to this message than he had to anything else I'd tried to say about the case. "Come on over here," he demanded, "and I'll tell you how to handle her next time."

That first plane trip to Madrid was the start of what turned out to be an almost daily commuter run from London. On the initial trip the rain in Spain was virtually continual. The mud was ankle deep and *Camelot* was a mess. When I met him, Richard was decked out in full armor for his role of King Arthur. But the armor was so heavy the crew had to just lay him down in the mud between takes, which caused considerable laughter whenever the shout went out, "It's time to lay the King!"

I stood there in the rain trying to talk with him, but it wasn't very satisfactory. Finally, Richard said, "Damn it, it's no good with you up there and me down here shouting so everybody can hear us. Come on, get down here where we can talk."

So I spent the next two hours sprawled in the mud of Madrid, carrying on an unbelievably disjointed conversation, punctuated by continual interruptions when the crew came to lift Richard up for another take before the cameras.

"Tell me exactly what she said," Richard urged.

"She didn't have anything to say."

"But how did she say it?"

"She said, 'Tell Richard it just won't work.' "

"No, no, not the words. What was her tone of voice?"

At that point the discussion was halted as the crew hoisted Richard upright, hosed off the mud and put him back before the cameras. After the scene was shot, we settled back into the mud again, and he continued, "You said that she was interested. I knew she would be."

"*I* didn't say that. You said it."

"Well, of course. I know her better than you. Did you tell her I would be willing to forgive her everything?"

"She said she wouldn't forgive *you* anything."

"Why should she? I didn't do anything."

I told Richard that Elizabeth had said that if he wanted to be forgiven, he could go to the other women he had betrayed.

"Ah! That's her big trouble," he said, happily. "She can't control her jealousy."

By the end of the day when I started for the airport, looking like an animated mud pie, Richard was still going strong, trying to perfect his personal script on "How to Handle a Woman."

"Now," he said, "this is what you tell her when you get back to London—"

"She doesn't want to talk to me again," I reminded him.

"Of course she does. If she didn't want to see you, she wouldn't have seen you the first time. Just do it the way I tell you, and she'll be eating out of your hand."

I felt she'd be more apt to break my arm if I even tried to extend my hand. To my surprise, though, Elizabeth did consent to see me again. But she still wanted no part of a reconciliation.

"We've played that," she said, "and it was a flop. Tell Richard to forget it."

I returned to Madrid the next day. The weather was so bad that filming had been suspended. I found Richard relaxing at the city's finest hotel in a suite amply stocked with his favorite foods—all liquid.

I had intended to return to London that evening, but Richard wouldn't hear of it. Using vodka bottles to illustrate, he painted a terrifying picture of the airliner struggling through the storm with ice forming on the wings, and the stark peaks of the Pyrenees looming out of the night.

"But you weren't on it," Richard said, waving his arms wildly. "I saved your life. I kept you here." And he did.

That night we went to Horcher's, one of Madrid's finest restaurants, but we had no reservations and took our place with about twenty others waiting for tables. Richard complained he was thirsty, and even a little hungry.

The maitre d' promised to send out a plate of hors d'oeuvres.

"And some drinks," Richard added.

"Most assuredly a drink."

Fifteen minutes passed with no sign of food or drink. The maitre d' was apologetic, "Unfortunately, none of the waiters are free at this time."

Richard told me to wait and disappeared into the rear. He reappeared in a few minutes with a towel draped over his arm, wearing a waiter's jacket and apron and carrying a huge tray full of hors d'oeuvres and wine. His balance was perfect, despite a good number of drinks consumed earlier, and he assumed the role with such professional aplomb that none of the other waiters questioned what was an apparently unannounced change in house policy. For almost half an hour, until our table was ready, Richard plied back and forth from the kitchen serving wine and hors d'oeuvres to everyone in the waiting area. When the maitre d' finally caught on, he and the other waiters were aghast but undeniably fascinated by Richard's sense of humor.

Back in the hotel room, Richard put on a totally madcap show for me, one of the greatest and longest one-man performances I've ever seen. He recited poetry, played scenes from a dozen plays, and, in between, discussed philosophy and life with Elizabeth. One minute he would rage about the disgraceful way she treated him, the next he would plead for ways to convince her that they must reconcile.

When the weather broke on Sunday and I was able to escape, he sent me back to London with the plea, "When you see her, tell her I'm willing to forgive everything. Remind her I've suffered, too— each of us has to pay for pleasure with pain."

I considered it hopeless but, after all, Richard was my client and was asking me to seek a reconciliation in his behalf.

I called on Elizabeth again, and this time found her more receptive than in earlier meetings. Her solicitor, she said, had explained to her that I was performing a professional duty.

But she was still adamant. No reconciliation. "It is just impossible," she said. "It wouldn't work, and you can tell him so."

I pressed for reasons on why she was so certain and repeated Richard's assurances of love, forgiveness, and repentance.

"I've heard all that before," she said wearily. "I'm going through with the divorce."

Her mind was made up, she said. Richard had placed his career above everything, leaving her to bear and raise his children while he rocketed about the world taking his fun where he found it. Gossip columnists constantly reported his amorous escapades and appetite for liquor. The long separations had made them virtual strangers.

I was off again to Spain the next morning to inform Richard I had done my best and failed. I told him Elizabeth would not change her mind.

"In that case," he said, still in armor and very much caught up in his role, "it will be a battle to the death!"

This essentially ended my role in Richard Harris's personal drama, except for one final appearance in his behalf. He was scheduled to appear in a London court the following Monday for a hearing on the issue of providing temporary support pending full trial of the divorce action. But the unseasonably wet Spanish weather had put the filming of *Camelot* so far behind schedule that Richard wanted to postpone the hearing so the crew could take full advantage of the clearing skies—in case the rain started up again. He asked me to carry this message back to his barristers since I was returning to London anyway.

I arrived barely in time to tell them before court convened. When the judge, bewigged and berobed as any "fossil" of Richard's imagination, took the bench, his barrister addressed the judge in that formal fashion which still governs English judicial procedure. "Milord," he said, "I crave leave of the court to permit Mr. Harris's California solicitor, Mr. Mitchelson, who just flew in from Spain and has a message from Mr. Harris, to address the court."

Milord, the judge, peered over his spectacles, and in his most lordly British manner said: "I will now hear from Mr. Mitchelson."

My borrowed robe and wig were at the ready, and I quickly donned them with the help of the junior barrister seated next to me and stood up. In a not so English manner but as carefully as possible, I said: "Milord, Mr. Harris wishes me to inform the court that most regrettably the rain in Spain, which normally falls mainly on the plain, has instead fallen mainly on location where they are attempting to film the motion picture *Camelot* in which Mr. Harris plays the title role of King Arthur. As the film company is most behind in their schedule, Mr. Harris and the director, Mr. Josh Logan, would be most appreciative if the court could grant Mr. Harris a two-week continuance so they can make up the lost time. However, if the court cannot grant this request, Mr. Harris will enplane for London this afternoon and be ready to proceed on arrival."

The continuance was granted, and as I left the court I couldn't help but think from Alan Jay Lerner to Richard Harris, *Camelot* was still with me.

This, as well as other cases, has made me realize that reconciliation is an area where most divorce lawyers do not excel. Despite many attempts through the years, I have had only occasional success, for by the time a person reaches the stage of consulting an attorney, the marriage has usually deteriorated to a point beyond repair. The spouses have already consulted friends, relatives, clergymen, and often, marriage counselors and psychiatrists as well.

I do make a point of asking clients if they are absolutely sure that things cannot be worked out. Often women who are served divorce papers without warning ask me to try and effect a reconciliation. But the reaction is usually caused by disbelief and occurs when the woman is emotionally unprepared to believe that her husband is serious. She usually loses the desire for getting back together once the initial shock wears off.

Efforts toward reconciliation after a divorce action has been initiated is a controversial subject. Society and the law are still dedicated to the preservation of marriage, especially where children are involved. Many states have laws that require pretrial conciliation efforts or cooling-off periods before the final decrees are granted. Some require a couple to consult with court-appointed marriage counselors or a conciliation service within the court itself. In other states the judges call the parties into chambers and try to act as marriage counselors before the trial begins. The result of such activities is inconclusive. The conciliation agencies (most of which operate at the taxpayers' expense) maintain glowing statistical records of their successes. Naturally, the follow-through on how long the "reconciliations" last is far less enthusiastically pursued.

Entertainer Mort Sahl has filed at least three divorce petitions against actress China Lee in less than two years. None have gone to trial, so at least some of them must be bouncing around as "reconciliation" statistics by now. Actress Mara Corday must have provided statistics for at least ten successful "reconciliations" with actor Richard Long before his death.

Some wives, and occasionally husbands, use divorce lawyers as a weapon in the battle of the sexes. They aren't really divorce clients or even potential divorce clients, because they have never sat down and made a reasoned decision to end their marriages. They simply rush from the latest heated quarrel, with bruised egos and wounded feelings, to find the nearest divorce lawyer. The papers, which they always demand be filed immediately, merely serve as instruments to bring their mates back into line. Serious divorce clients, on the other hand, make their decision to file only after long consideration.

For many years in California, reconciliation efforts were required by law. That law saved very few marriages, but it managed to complicate a lot of divorce cases. When either a wife or husband indicated a willingness to "talk out" the differences, the judge interrupted the proceedings and sent them both for marriage counseling.

The absurdity sometimes resulting from this mandatory requirement was well illustrated during the divorce trial of Craig and Lee Ann Breedlove, who were about the fastest people alive. They had been a car-racing couple, and, at the time, my client Craig held the men's world land-speed record and Lee Ann held the women's. When Lee Ann was asked if she did, or wished to, consult with the court's marriage counselor, she replied, "No ... I don't think it would do any good in this case, since my husband has remarried." Craig, living up to his reputation for speed, had obtained a Nevada divorce after Lee Ann filed—and was sitting in the courtroom with his new bride.

CHAPTER ELEVEN

The Equal Division of Unequal Earnings

Prenuptial agreements are rather anachronistic contracts with which divorce lawyers still have to deal on occasion, especially in community property states. They are perfectly legal if they meet all the provisions required for a valid contract and are not contrary to public policy. But they are rarely fair.

Basically, such agreements attempt to exclude one spouse from sharing the other's wealth or property in the event of a divorce. Shortly after property rights for women became broadly recognized early in this century, the agreements had a brief heyday, as the American dream of poor but pretty shop girls marrying into wealth became a popular reality. Their use declined, however, when the courts ignored the premarriage contracts and awarded women enough alimony to keep them from becoming public charges.

But premarital pacts are still made occasionally, usually by the extremely wealthy or by figures in the entertainment world, whose monetary and marital positions are frequently mercurial. The victim—the one who waives the rights to claims on the other's wealth—is usually the woman who seldom fully understands what she is doing or is too much in love to care. Most women have no real concept of the extent of their marital rights. They think the prenuptial agreement means each will keep what belonged to the individual before the marriage, which seems only fair, and not give up any property rights acquired during the marriage—although that is, in fact, the purpose of most such documents. They only discover the full meaning of the agreement much later, when one partner wants out. That's also the time when many men use the document as a weapon to bring their wives back under control and keep them subservient.

Ellen Drew was one of those pre-World War II Hollywood Cinderellas who was discovered by a Paramount talent scout behind the counter of a local candy shop. She had gotten some good parts, including a major role in the Bing Crosby-Fred MacMurray musical, *Sing, You Sinners,* but when the war broke out she married Sy Bartlett, a writer-producer now an Air Corps officer, and dropped out of films to play the role of service wife.

After the war she returned to acting and was divorced from Bartlett in 1949. In 1951, her career was again on the rise when she signed a prenuptial agreement before marrying her second husband, William T. Walker, a multimillionaire who described himself as a "retired financier." Although Louella Parsons reported the romance and wrote "Ellen will not be giving up her career," the actress did, in fact, make one more picture before disappearing from public view for sixteen years.

It was a simple document Ellen Drew laid in front of me at our initial meeting. "In consideration of $10, paid in hand," Ellen had waived all her marital property rights. It also stated that each party would retain, separately, any earnings gained during the marriage. She told me other lawyers insisted it couldn't be broken, but after studying the document, I disagreed and decided to take her case. In filing the suit I charged the usual mental cruelty, completely ignoring the prenuptial agreement. Walker promptly countersued and naturally, on the basis of the prenuptial agreement, claimed that the house and everything else he possessed was his own separate property. There was no immediate move on either party's part to oust the other from possession, as is so often the case.

There are sound psychological reasons why people wish to remain in their homes when they are going through a divorce.

Their worlds are turned upside down, and their home becomes something of an island of comfort in the sea of confusion. In Ellen's case, eviction would have dealt a double psychological blow—not only casting her adrift at a time of great fear and anxiety but also suggesting to her the prenuptial agreement's possible effect on her whole life. On the other hand, Walker, too, would be upset and outraged at the thought of being deprived of something he considered his "separate property"—something he had taken pains to protect.

With both Ellen and Walker each occupying separate wings (such are the benefits of wealth), it should have worked as well as any other awkward arrangement, for the home had been designed with "his" and "her" wings, leaving only a common front entrance, kitchen, and, of course, a single swimming pool and patio area. But it didn't.

Placing people who can no longer tolerate each other in close proximity is like putting a torch near a leaking gas line. The slightest breeze can cause an explosion, and this one wasn't long in coming. Within a few days Ellen was at my office in a state bordering on hysteria. The night before, when she was on her way to her room, Walker had stood at the dividing line and repeatedly clicked the hammer of a revolver pointed in her general direction. She wasn't sure if he meant to harm her or just warn her of what might be in store for her, but she was clearly terrified.

I immediately petitioned the court for a hearing to demand that Walker be tossed out of the house. My associate, Harold Rhoden, and I also filed a separate one million dollar damage suit against Walker for assault.

I wasn't really sure if the court would order Walker from the house, since his explanation that he'd planned to go hunting and was just testing an empty weapon had a certain plausibility. But we decided to go through with a full hearing to impress upon him that we wouldn't tolerate any more moves to harass and intimidate Ellen. Besides, we felt that a handgun was an unconvincing hunting piece. At any rate, the assault suit was an insurance policy against such harassment.

After a two-day hearing, the judge refused to put Walker out of the house, but he did limit his movements so drastically that it proved to be a potent element in convincing him to seek a settlement of the property dispute. Walker ended up being restricted to his own room, ordered to use the back entrance, and allowed kitchen privileges only from 7 A.M. to 8 A.M.

While the skirmishes were being fought, Walker and his lawyers still contended that the prenuptial agreement was valid. They also claimed that there was no community property because Walker had lived off his stock investments all during the marriage and there had been no community earnings.

I considered the prenuptial agreement invalid for two, or possibly three, legal reasons. In the first place, I discovered Walker had overlooked a small but vital detail—he never gave Ellen the $10 at the time she signed the agreement. With a millionaire's casualness about small change, he contended it was just a formality that didn't mean anything. While in one sense it might have seemed a trivial point, the contract had plainly been executed without full consideration, and it is on such apparently small points that big cases often turn.

I also believed that Walker had breached the contract when he made Ellen stop working after the marriage, since a major portion of the agreement provided that each keep his or her earnings separate. How could one have any earnings if not permitted to work? That was the clause that actually purported to nullify her community property rights, since everything her husband had at the time they married was legally his separate property, even without the agreement.

There was some question, too, of whether she had really understood what she had signed, even though she had had independent legal advice. It was a weaker argument, but I thought there was some merit to the fact that she was "in love" and under "undue influence" by nature of the great trust she then had in Walker.

I also felt we had a good position against his contention that there were no community earnings during the marriage. He was one of those investors who managed his own stock portfolio and, therefore, we contended that a great deal of his $3.5 million in assets, acquired during the sixteen years of marriage, was a result of his community "efforts and services," which should entitle Ellen to a share of it.

His lawyers never showed any real interest in settlement until the judge, as it were, kept Walker in his room for being a bad boy. After that, Walker couldn't wait to get Ellen out of the house, and he was willing to make almost any reasonable compromise to accomplish this.

In the end, the prenuptial aggreement wasn't actually declared invalid because it wasn't litigated. However, I consider that it was, in fact, broken by the terms of a rather generous negotiated settlement that we worked out shortly before the trial started. It became just another scrap of paper when Walker's attorneys agreed that Ellen was entitled to a share of the community property and compensation for her lost earning capacity. We made some concessions also, among them, the dismissal of the assault suit.

Another prenuptial agreement that was never really broken because the case was settled before the issue was litigated involved rock star Johnny Rivers and his lovely, sad-eyed wife, Vicky. I was brought into the case by one of my former associates, Marty Klass. I found myself involved with the wildly chaotic world of rock music where the only reality is what conventional people would consider the unreal, a fantastic substrata where millions are made overnight by musicians barely old enough to get an after-school job in a fast-food restaurant. Where at thirty, you're not just old, you're practically dead—in the business, that is.

Johnny Rivers had come out of Tennessee. At twenty-five he was a pencil-thin, millionaire superstar with a scraggly beard and moustache who had five-figure recording contracts and hit records banging out of every juke box. He also had a sullen and suspicious nature and was determined nobody was going to get his money or tell him what to do.

Vicky was slim, sleek, and cool, with the fragile kind of beauty one finds on the cover of *Vogue*. A shy, rather introverted woman, she came from a conservative family and had been trained in business college as a secretary. In fact, Marty told me she once worked in my office for a few days but that I had not found her satisfactory and let her go. I sure couldn't remember it, though, and don't see how I could have either forgotten or fired such a lovely lady.

Somehow, she caught the eye of the "Great Johnny Rivers," who, like most rock stars, was constantly surrounded by hordes of adoring females, all eager to be with him. He chose Vicky, and in no time she was pregnant.

At first he tried to convince her to have an abortion. When she continued to refuse, he finally consented to marry her, only if she signed a prenuptial agreement. Later, when I asked why he'd insisted on the agreement, his answer was typically Johnny Rivers: "Nobody's gonna take what I worked for away from me. I made it and it's mine."

He was absolutely right. By law, everything he had at the time of the marriage was his own separate property and would remain so as long as he didn't co-mingle it with community assets or give it away. But he didn't need a prenuptial agreement to protect it.

Vicky, however, signed the agreement; they got married, and their son was born. Once the baby came, she told me, Rivers was crazy about him.

The marriage lasted about eighteen months, during which time Johnny went to the top. He had his own music company. He was a major owner of the Fifth Dimension, a hugely successful rock group. And he made more than a million dollars.

Toward Vicky he conducted himself like a combination Caesar-Napoleon. Vicky was married but that didn't necessarily mean he was. His basic premise was that whatever he did was right because he did it. He could choose any woman he wanted to be with and spend his money on anything he wished. As he told Vicky, "It's none of your business what I do, where I go, or who I see. Nobody tells me what to do."

As a result of this treatment, Vicky fell into fits of deep depression. When friends asked why she didn't divorce him, she replied, "He said if I tried, he'd take the baby and leave me without a penny."

I was fairly sure we could break the prenuptial agreement on grounds that she was pregnant at the time she signed it and therefore under duress and that she received legal advice from an attorney chosen by her husband. It was in this positive state of mind that I started taking Johnny's pretrial deposition.

At the time, Johnny was into a health food kick and he arrived at my office with a big thermos of herb tea, a bag of alfalfa sprouts, and other such delicacies. He sat there with his lawyer, sipping his tea, while Marty and I questioned him about the prenuptial agreement. Originally, three copies of the prenuptial agreement had been prepared and signed. Two copies had been accounted for. Neither had been given to Vicky. I asked what had been done with the original copy.

It is a fundamental rule of contracts that all parties to an agreement must be delivered copies of it. The reason is plain. If one party had all the copies, he could doctor or rewrite the agreement. I felt I was on the right track when his lawyer instructed Johnny not to answer. But, "Nobody tells Johnny Rivers what to do," and he told me the original was still in his business lawyer's safe.

His lawyer objected vehemently that Johnny had no way of knowing the answer, that he was just guessing and demanded that the response be stricken from the record. But Johnny had put his finger in it—right up to his elbow. Obviously, if Vicky had never been delivered a copy, the prenuptial agreement, by that fact alone, was probably invalid.

I suggested that since the other lawyer's office coincidentally was right next door to mine, on the same floor, the simple solution would be for us to check his safe. When he objected, I reminded him that it would be possible to go before the court and get a discovery order requiring it. But Marty suggested we call a presiding judge of the Domestic Relations Court whom we all knew, and settle it right then rather than go through the formal motion.

Johnny's lawyer said there was no precedent for getting an oral court order in the middle of a deposition.

The judge, of course, agreed he couldn't issue an order over the telephone, but added he could see no reason why there was any objection to looking in the safe in the interest of clearing the air and speeding up matters. Either the document was there or it was not, and looking for it now could prevent possible charges later that evidence had been removed or destroyed. He also indicated he would be available for any formal motion, if we found we could not agree.

Johnny's lawyer was between a rock and hard place. He could insist on a formal order, but the judge had already given what was, in effect, a tentative ruling by indicating how he would act. We three lawyers went to the next office to inspect the safe. The original copy was there, which made the so-called prenuptial agreement no longer the original issue in the case.

When we got back to my office Johnny was nowhere to be found. We finally located him in the bathroom. His lawyer told him to come out.

"I won't!" he shouted through the door. "I'm meditating!"

The case was finally settled at the courthouse door, giving Vicky a settlement which gave her custody of the child, ample child support, and about a quarter of a million dollars in alimony.

Even under the best of circumstances, marriage is difficult but when it starts out under the handicap of a prenuptial agreement, it's comparable to a funeral oration at the wedding ceremony—a tacit confession by one party that the marriage is probably doomed before it starts. If one of the parties is that apprehensive before the vows are taken, the marriage probably has little chance of success. The prenuptial agreement is also almost always against the interests of the woman, placing her in a position of dependence from the start. In such cases, the agreement then becomes a weapon used to continue a relationship long after its vitality has ended and it can become a way of compelling almost involuntary servitude.

CHAPTER TWELVE

To Have and to Hold

Custody battles are a problem divorce lawyers must contend with rather frequently, though they are viewed with very little pleasure. Custody is an area of domestic relations law where emotions run highest, everybody gets hurt, and nobody wins.

Under Roman law, children, like all other property, belonged to the man, since he was head of the family. It was a policy based on economics: children could work and produced income. Only in the past hundred years, since the Industrial Revolution shifted the emphasis from rural to urban society, has the idea become popular that mothers should be given custody.

The new social sciences, psychology and sociology, stressed the importance of a mother's love and care to the point where social mores rendered it almost axiomatic that women should have custody of children, unless there was solid proof of moral or mental unfitness.

Currently, the pendulum is swinging in the other direction, propelled by changing assessments of the same social sciences and by the feminist revolution. Psychological and sociological absolutes of yesterday are now relative. Children are not necessarily better off in the care of their mothers. Today more and more women are rejecting motherhood and homemaking as their chief functions in life and are gladly ceding custody to their ex-husbands.

Still, in the majority of divorce cases where there are minor children, custody remains a major issue. The courts, which are usually invoked to decide who should have the offspring, tend to go along with this psychological-sociological trend—sometimes even deciding that the child's welfare is best served in the custody of a third party.

The elimination of "fault" in the grounds for divorce in California and other progressive states has stopped much of the sordid tattling in the divorce part of the case but not necessarily in the custody phase, where tales of marital misconduct are often material to determine both parental fitness and the child's best interests. Such washing of dirty linen in the legal laundromat is increasingly frowned upon, however. Fortunately, many parents now are beginning to realize that such actions in custody fighting come close to destroying their children as well as themselves. Today there is somewhat of a new spirit of compromise evolving among both lawyers and their clients in the direction of negotiating custody agreements. While custody is supposed to be awarded solely on the basis of "the best interests of the child," most judges will accept any reasonable agreement reached by the parents.

But when I first started practicing law, custody fights were common. They were also bitter, sometimes bizarre, and often never-ending. One of my earliest cases combined all three elements.

I was one of the attorneys who represented actor Sterling Hayden's ex-wife, Betty, in her futile attempt to keep him from taking their four children to Tahiti aboard an aging two-masted sailing schooner. The Haydens had been through a headline-grabbing divorce and a series of custody skirmishes long before I entered the case. The children had been in Sterling's custody for more than two years before Betty asked for my help in blocking the South Seas voyage.

Though he had custody of the children, Hayden was prohibited from removing them from California without the court's permission. He had filed a petition to get this approval for the voyage, but Betty felt that both the trip and the old windjammer were too dangerous for the children, the oldest of them being only ten. At the time, we filed a petition seeking an order restraining Hayden from taking the children on the intended voyage. At the same time we asked that custody be modified to give the children back to Betty. The move started one of the longest and most bitter custody battles in Los Angeles Court history.

The hearing opened in the old Hall of Records, the last of the original civic center buildings in Los Angeles (since torn down). Midway through the trial, which lasted almost eight weeks, the new civil courthouse opened, and we moved to one of the more spacious and modern courtrooms to become the first trial in the new building.

Both parents were acting in what they believed was the best interest of their offspring. Hayden was a good, devoted father who wanted to be with his children and felt they were better off with him. At the time, however, he was having some identity problems because, as he said in his own autobiography, he couldn't identify with the Hollywood scene and was ashamed to accept its money.

While he saw nothing dangerous about the proposed voyage, even for young children, Betty believed the old schooner was unsafe. I think she also had some reservations about Hayden's ability to handle the vessel through such a long voyage, despite the fact that he held Master Mariner papers and had been running away to sea ever since he was a boy when things got too difficult for him on land.

We spent most of the trial pointing out the dangers to young children inherent in such a long voyage and attacking the sea-worthiness of a sixty-five-year-old vessel that had once been ship-wrecked. (I have since been told that a few years later the bottom fell out of the ship while it was tied up at a dock in Sausalito, California.)

Because of the custody change issue, Hayden and his lawyers spent the rest of the trial attacking Betty's moral character and personal life. Without doubt she was one of the most indestructible clients I've ever had. Her ex-husband and his lawyers brought in numerous people to testify about her personal life and conduct in an attempt to deny her custody. In turn we questioned some of Hayden's political affiliations.

One day Hayden's main lawyer, a man with a formidable reputation who always sought to intimidate us by hinting that the worst was yet to come, cornered me in the hall and hinted at still more forthcoming allegations, which I knew couldn't be true since they never happened. It was this incident, as much as his general demeanor, that led me to challenge the testimony of a Hayden witness I've always called "the detective on a box."

He was a little man, no more than five foot five, with a little man's tendency to be overassertive. On the witness stand, he read names, dates, and incidents out of a little black book with the clipped precision of a Marine drill instructor. His stories of Betty's alleged amorous activities, supposedly observed by peering through her windows, were detailed, complete, and unbelievable.

After we adjourned for the day, I went to Betty's home up in the Hollywood Hills to familiarize myself with the premises in preparation for cross-examination. What I discovered sent me in pursuit of a copy of the house blueprint and a photographer. There wasn't a single window in the house with a sill less than six-and-a-half-feet from the ground! In addition, only one window, on the north side, gave any view of Betty's bed at all—and it was partially obscured even when the shade, curtains, and drapes were wide open.

The next morning I arrived at court with copies of the blueprints and a series of photographs, which we had worked all night to develop. After pinning the blueprints on the courtroom blackboard, I started my cross-examination.

"Just how were you able to make these observations?" I asked the short detective.

"I sneaked up to the window from behind a tree."

"And you stood on the ground outside looking inside?"

"Yes."

"And was it the north window you were looking in?"

He flipped through the pages of his little black book, stuck out his jaw, and answered, "That's right, the north window."

I introduced a photograph of the north window. After he identified it as the window he had peered through, I asked him how tall he stood. Hayden's lawyer objected on the grounds it was immaterial, but was overruled by the judge. After the detective answered, I introduced a photograph of the north window with a tape measure hanging from the sill.

"As you can see," I said, "this window is more than six feet from the ground where you told me you stood. How could you see into the room?"

He seemed to lose some of his cockiness. "I must have my directions wrong," he answered defensively. "I was looking downtown, so it must have been the west window."

"You mean to tell me you were really standing on the ground outside the west window?"

But he wasn't going to be caught twice. "Not on the ground. I stood on a box."

"Where did you get the box?"

"From my car."

"You mean you carried a box all the way from your car?"

"It wasn't heavy. It was a cardboard box."

That brought a smile from the judge.

Then I produced photographs to show there wasn't any bedroom window on the west side. That drew more chuckles from the bench. We went through a similar routine for the south wall, working almost all the way around the house. The south window photographs showed the bedroom couldn't be seen at all. By then everyone in the courtroom was breaking up—including Hayden and his lawyers.

We clearly won that round but failed in our bid to shift custody, though the judge did order Hayden not to take the children on the Tahiti voyage. It turned out to be a hollow victory for Betty, however, because Hayden defied the court order and sailed anyway.

When he returned some months later, the same judge gave him a lecture and suspended his contempt of court sentence. By having sailed in open defiance of the court, Hayden was saying, I don't care what the court or the law says. I was rather disturbed about it at the time and felt that permitting such open defiance, brought discredit on both the court and our legal system. However, the judge stated, in effect, that he felt Hayden was acting out of frustration (rather than intentional disrespect for the court) since Betty had been harassing Hayden from the time of their divorce with repetitious court proceedings.

When it comes to marathon custody battles, however, I don't think any child has been fought for more often, or more publicly, than Christian Devi Brando, son of Marlon Brando and Anna Kashfi. They were divorced when the boy was an infant, and by the time he was fourteen each parent had won custody at least twice in a series of bitter and highly publicized custody trials.

I became involved in a somewhat backdoor fashion which stemmed from representing Anna in a traffic matter. First arrested for drunk driving, she was later booked for driving under the influence of drugs when chemical tests showed she had not been drinking. Actually, neither substance was responsible for her apparent unsteady condition. Showing me an ugly scar on her leg, she told me she was suffering from the effects of a bite by the rare and deadly Brown Recluse Spider. It was an unusual story, but incredibly enough, I suffered the same painful bite sometime later myself and as a result was hospitalized for two weeks. Medical records and statements from toxicologists backed up her claim. After an independent investigation, the prosecuting attorney agreed with the findings, and the charges were dismissed.

Later Anna asked me for help with the custody problem. What had happened was that after fourteen years of battling, Brando had custody under an agreement that virtually barred Anna from seeing her son at all. Many lawyers had told her the agreement with Brando was "unbreakable," although "unbreakable" agreements are considered a trial lawyer's Mount Everest.

I was curious to meet Brando and find out firsthand what kind of a man would try to prevent a mother from even *seeing* her only son. I only knew the public image—that of a brooding, introverted man subject to the kind of idiosyncrasies that would compel him to refuse an Academy Award on the grounds that movies unfairly depicted the life and times of the American Indian—and then send a self-styled Indian princess to the ceremonies as his spokeswoman.

Seeking to reopen the custody issue, I drew up a petition which included all the basic charges, plus the fact that Anna was denied all visiting rights. And I added an allegation which I think was unprecedented at that time. I charged that Brando's role in a controversial film, newly released, made him unfit to retain custody of the boy. Anna's petition stated:

> ... In *Last Tango in Paris,* Mr. Brando performs a role of a sexually maladjusted and perverted person, wherein he exhibits himself in various stages of nudity and simulated sex acts. ...
>
> Throughout the film [he] utters obscene, foul, shocking, and distasteful profanities. As a result thereof, my son has been subject to ridicule and embarrassment. ...

The petition also touched on the Academy Award incident:

> Because of Mr. Brando's recent radical and unsocial behavior, together with his immoral and unconventional conduct in general, an unhealthy climate and atmosphere have been created which cannot escape the attention of my son. ...

The next problem was serving the papers on Brando in order to bring him before the court. His attorneys of record told me they were not authorized to accept service on the actor's behalf. To a former process server this provided an interesting challenge.

I had Brando's Mulholland Drive estate staked out and kept under constant surveillance. Brando was seen on the premises, but the process servers could find no way of getting through to him.

I then hired a helicopter to make an aerial reconnaissance and found a process server intrigued enough by both the idea and the fee to be willing to drop out of the sky. We knew it would be a one-shot ploy with no chance of a rerun, so we planned carefully. The plan was simple. We would develop "engine trouble" over the estate, flutter down for an emergency landing; the process server would hop out and serve Brando when he rushed out to see what was happening.

The plan was a good one—except that when the chopper fluttered down for the emergency landing Brando didn't materialize, though the front door was open. But my process server was of the kind of caliber that would have been tough competition for me in the old days. (In fact, he was the son of the man who originally trained me.) Resourceful to the end, he walked through the open door, found Brando in a bedroom, thrust the papers into the shocked actor's hands, did an about-face, and casually walked back out the door. The whole thing was over in about a minute, and the helicopter went clacking its way back to the airport.

An hour later the attorneys called to tell me that Brando had informed them he intended to represent himself in the new custody fight and that I would be hearing from him directly. This created a new dilemma. No attorney cares to deal directly with the other party in such actions, not only because of the emotions involved, but because any agreement is subject to a later charge that the attorney took advantage of the party's legal ignorance and exercised undue influence.

When Brando called I urged him to get legal counsel, both for his sake and Anna's, but he insisted on trying to "talk it out" first. Reluctantly I agreed, but only after a written exchange outlining ground rules and stating the reasons I considered he should have an attorney.

The first meeting was short and nonproductive. I guess we were primarily trying to take each other's measure. He came in Levis and T-shirt and, speaking in his familiar cynical monotone, launched into a tirade on how "fed up and disgusted" he was with lawyers who had "caused most of our problems and only cared about their fees."

At the next meeting, when he started on the same theme, I interrupted to say the issue concerned a woman's right to see her son—not lawyers or their fees. Brando suddenly dropped his cynicism and became both sincere and forthright. With actors one never knows what is real and what is role, but it didn't matter because the sincere and forthright Brando became the one I had to deal with.

For the rest of that meeting, and in several subsequent meetings, we had some long, down-to-earth conversations. Not all of them were related to the custody issue, though he did tell me in detail about the marriage, divorce, and the bitter court battles through the years.

"None of that's important now," he drawled. "What's best for our son is all that counts."

I reminded him it was also necessary to consider Anna's rights, but he insisted he hadn't taken any rights from her and started to review the fourteen years of the case. I stopped him. "We can match press clippings on the history of this case, but that won't solve anything," I said.

Despite the number of conferences and some interesting side discussions on subjects ranging from Shakespeare to the state of the economy, a week before the date of the hearing we still had no agreement. Then Anna, under great strain and tension, was hospitalized for both physical and emotional exhaustion.

When I called Brando to tell him why the hearing would have to be postponed, he asked how he could help. I told him, "You could lighten her emotional burden. As things stand, Anna is exiled from a son she loves very much, and the separation is half of her current problem."

Both he and Christian Devi visited her at the hospital, and within a short time Brando and I worked out a new agreement which allowed him to keep custody but restored Anna's visiting rights—with the boy's wishes held as a primary consideration.

The old theories of custody die hard, probably because most parents find it difficult to truly abandon the concept that children are property. "My baby" or "my son" is still very much a part of the average parent's vocabulary, and each parent naturally tends to think *his* or *her* love and companionship is the most important thing for the child's best interests, even in cases where an impartial third party might conclude that neither parent is truly fit. However, society, the law, and the courts are reluctant about separating children from their natural parents, except in extreme circumstances. Consequently, most judicial custody orders represent attempts to minimize the adverse effects on all parties involved and sometimes result in bizarre and painful aftereffects. This makes out-of-court custody agreements more important, in my opinion, than out-of-court property and alimony settlements. An amicable custody agreement, like the one worked out between Brando and Anna, although late in coming in this particular case, is more likely to be observed by both parents because each party is satisfied about its fairness. On the other hand, one or both parties usually feel they've been discriminated against after a bitter custody battle before the judge—and the "losing" party too often takes it into his or her own hands to "correct" the alleged miscarriage of justice. This can lead to an illegal solution which lawyers, judges, and all those connected with the administration of the judicial system dread most—the so-called "child snatch."

CHAPTER THIRTEEN

Children, Let Us Away

What remains at the conclusion of most custody battles is pain to all the parties involved, but even more devastating results take place when one party refuses to accept the court's judgment or becomes disenchanted with a custody agreement. Under these circumstances, the unhappy parent sometimes unwittingly becomes a criminal by a series of actions in which he may grab the child and flee, pursued by police and private detectives, by court orders and writs, by unhappy ex-spouses and the ever-present unpredictable operations of fate.

The transcontinental and even transoceanic "child snatch" escapades that issue from these situations occur because of a unique exception to the U.S. Constitutional requirement that each state must recognize and enforce the legal decisions of other states (the full faith and credit clause). Custody cases are excluded from this law because these judgments are never considered final or permanent by the court, any more than they are by the parents.

This open-ended position was intended for the child's protection. A child is unable to protect himself, and the conditions of the custody situation sometimes change overnight. Consequently, the courts take the position that if there has been a change of circumstances, they have a right to hear about it if the child is living within their jurisdiction (although courts will also often refer a matter back to the court of original jurisdiction). This frequently makes the task of bringing the "stolen" child back extraordinarily difficult, expensive, and time-consuming. Sometimes, it makes it impossible.

Many people equate child snatching with kidnapping and can't understand why a lawyer doesn't immediately obtain a warrant and call in the FBI. But it's impossible to "kidnap" your own child. Criminal charges of child stealing could be filed, but many courts will not entertain any criminal charges in these cases because the child's parent is involved. Courts prefer to handle these incidents as a contempt of a civil court order when some form of punishment is considered necessary. In the Hayden case, there was an attempt to invoke criminal statutes mainly in the hope of persuading federal or French authorities to intervene. However, both sides chose to treat it as a civil custody matter, and even the California authorities dropped the criminal charges once Hayden returned with the children.

Early in my career I handled a child-snatching case that is still one of the most complex, multi-jurisdictional domestic relations cases I've ever encountered.

Saliha Hassan was a sultry, dark-haired woman who managed a fashionable Beverly Hills boutique. Her first words when she came to my office were, "My ex-husband has stolen my son."

As the daughter of a Turkish senator, Saliha worked in Ankara as an interpreter at the American Aid Mission, which was where she first met Air Force Master Sergeant Lester J. Martin. Romance blossomed and she followed Martin to Germany, where they were married. Their son, Robert Glenn, was born in Austria shortly before Martin was transferred back to the United States and stationed at Ellsworth Air Force Base in South Dakota. Like many career military men, however, Martin maintained as legal residence his boyhood home, a small town near Jackson, Tennessee.

After three years, the marriage broke up. Saliha obtained a Nevada divorce and was given legal custody of her son. She later moved to Los Angeles and married a local importer. She was in the process of divorcing her second husband, primarily because of his attitude toward her child, when Martin showed up on an extended leave with a request to visit his son.

"I had no objections," Saliha told me. "I felt it would be good for Bobbie and his father to get to know each other. I arranged with my housekeeper for the visits, and Lester came every day for about a week. Then one day he said I wasn't caring for Bobbie properly because I was working. He said he wanted to take him."

"What did you tell him?"

"I said the court had given me custody, that he had agreed to it, and he couldn't have him, and if that was how he felt, he couldn't visit any more. He left the house quite angry."

She told me he had come back again the day before our meeting, picked up the child, and told the housekeeper he was taking the boy to the movies.

"When I came home," she said, "they still hadn't returned. And when I called his hotel, they said he had checked out, and that he had a child with him."

She hadn't notified the police, so the first thing I did was to call them and ask that a warrant be issued for Martin, on the remote chance that he hadn't left the state yet. While Saliha signed the complaint, I called the base in South Dakota where Martin was stationed and found he still had several weeks of leave and had not yet reported back. I was fairly certain Martin had taken the child to his mother's home in Tennessee.

Saliha wanted to know what we could do next. I told her we could start an action in California or go to Tennessee with the Nevada divorce papers and ask their courts to act on the basis of them.

She nodded. "Let's go," she said.

For a moment I had some second thoughts. I'd never heard of a custody case with so many potential jurisdictional problems. But that night we caught a flight to Jackson. The next morning I appeared at the courthouse—a California lawyer asking a Tennessee circuit judge to enforce a Nevada custody order between a Turkish citizen and a military man based in South Dakota. And I was asking on the mere suspicion that Martin was in the state.

The Southern authorities were polite but very distant and less than 100 percent responsive to my inquiries. As outsiders in a place where almost everyone seemed to have a kissin' kin connection, Saliha and I decided it might be wiser to find a local associate counsel. A series of courthouse inquiries turned up the name of Billy Jack Goodrich as the best man for our purpose.

After Billy Jack listened to our story, we went back to the courthouse where he easily obtained an order commanding Martin to turn the child over to Saliha. Now all we had to do was to find him and serve the paper. Billy Jack solved that, too, by calling on the local police. After a few minutes of first-name conversation, he learned that Martin was indeed back in town, though nobody had seen much of him except his oldest friend—who happened to be a cousin of one of the policemen.

We decided to use the State Police to serve the order. After a brief stake-out of the home of Martin's mother, we intercepted him, served the order, and took custody of the child, who was being kept at the old friend's home.

I returned to the hotel where Saliha was staying, delighted with the ease with which we had accomplished what I had anticipated as a difficult task, and the three of us prepared to take the next plane back to Los Angeles. However, this was not the slow-moving Southern town it appeared to be, and before we could check out, we were served with a court order forbidding us to remove the boy from its jurisdiction and commanding us to appear in court the following day.

I immediately met with Billy Jack. Both of us went over the documents and the relevant legal statutes, and I pointed out that we appeared to have the law on our side. Billy Jack nodded. "But Les Martin'll have the courtroom. You're not fieldin' much of a team. Les is a home-town boy. He's from an old family. He's in the military. What are you? You're a damn Yankee and from California, too. Mrs. Hassan's a foreigner." He leaned back in his chair, lit a cigar, and exhaled a cloud of blue smoke. "But people here are my folks, too, and I'd say we'll do all right."

The next morning the local papers had played up the story, and when we walked into the old-fashioned courthouse, its halls were packed with people who had come to watch the drama. We ran the gauntlet of cold stares as we filed into the court. When Martin arrived in fresh-pressed blues with rows of campaign ribbons on his chest, everybody in the room said hello to him. Even the judge nodded and smiled.

"They're going to take my boy," Saliha said.

Billy Jack gave her a reassuring smile. "They're only going to try, ma'am."

I didn't share his confidence.

Martin took the stand first. He only wanted custody, he said, because Saliha wasn't giving Bobbie proper care. His Southern accent, barely noticeable when I took the boy the previous day, had turned thick as molasses overnight. "Ah brought mah boy home wheah he could grow up like Ah did. Fishin', huntin', an' eatin' good Southern food. With mah own mother to rea' him up in a Bible-readin' home."

Sure, he'd agreed to let Saliha have custody. But he didn't expect her to take the child to a place like Los Angeles, then go to work and leave him alone all day. He knew he violated the law in taking him, but it was "fo' mah boy's own good."

During all his testimony, the most specific fact that Martin could give to explain Saliha's "neglect" was to say that "a woman who goes out workin' all day is neglectin' him." That hardly constituted a legal case, but it certainly posed an emotional one. As an attorney who on occasion had played that kind of hand successfully, I had little reason to be overconfident at this point.

Our turn came, and Billy Jack introduced our documents before putting Saliha on the stand to elicit testimony that Martin made no effort to see the child for more than two years after the divorce. It was also made clear that she fed and dressed Bobbie each morning, took him to school, and cared for him after work.

During final arguments, Martin's lawyer evoked the joys of youth amid the natural beauties of the Tennessee hills, adding that most any father would prefer that to the foul smog and depraved atmosphere of Los Angeles as a place in which to have his son grow up. The only thing wrong with his summation was that it didn't touch one legal issue involved in the case! What concerned me was that this might not matter.

Billy Jack didn't do much better at arguing the law. Though I thrust my legal notes into his hand as he rose to speak, he just glanced at them, shoved them into his pocket—then proceeded to eulogize motherhood until there was hardly a dry eye in the place. He did this until the judge recessed for lunch, announcing that he'd rule in the afternoon session.

At lunch Billy Jack returned my notes. "Judge Tip Taylor is one of the best in the state," he said. "No need to remind him of the law. He knew the law was on our side before the hearing started."

"But those summations," I said, "what did they really have to do with the case?"

"Nothing," he grinned. "But those folks all came for a show, and we couldn't disappoint them." He patted Saliha on the arm. "Don't you fret, Mrs. Hassan. You'll be taking your boy home with you."

The courtroom was still packed that afternoon. Judge Taylor took the bench and began discussing the importance of fatherhood and the privilege of being able to live in Tennessee.

Saliha looked anguished, and I began to have a sinking feeling in the pit of my stomach. Billy Jack seemed unconcerned.

Then the judge started talking about motherhood as a "sacred institution filled with joys and sorrows" and described his own mother as a "sweet, gentle woman at whose knee I learned right from wrong."

Finally, he got down to the decision. In just a few words, he quoted the controlling laws and declared that Saliha should retain custody.

"Mr. Mitchelson, we don't all deal with it the same way," Billy Jack said at the airport that night, "but the law's the law all over."

From my experience, I've learned that fathers are the most likely candidates for the child-snatching role. But in another of my early cases, it was the mother who played that role—not only once, but twice. In some ways it was like the Sterling Hayden case: the parent who had custody fled across the ocean into another jurisdiction. But Hayden did it openly, after a full court hearing. Mrs. Barbara Weyland Gardner just quietly vanished one day and took her daughter with her.

Barbara and David Weyland were two people who should never have married in the first place. He was a quiet young man from San Francisco, studious and introspective. He was just out of college, with an ROTC commission, when he met Barbara at a party given by a fellow officer. On the surface, Barbara was a lonely soldier's dream. She had a figure that induced wolf whistles and a manner that reminded people of Marilyn Monroe. A product of Hollywood, she had learned to read from movie fan magazines and had but one devouring ambition—to become a star. While waiting to be "discovered," she worked as a model and occasionally as a movie extra.

David fell for her instantly, and they married before he shipped out for Korea. When he came home Barbara still hadn't broken into the film industry, but she was still hoping. Then she discovered she was pregnant and the child, Wendy Diane, was born.

"By then," David told me later, "I realized that the baby was all we had in common, and before long she divided us even further."

Soon after the child was born, Barbara started making the rounds of the talent agencies with her, hoping to have Wendy appear in advertisements. It became her obsession—and another source of bickering between the parents.

When Wendy was two, the Weylands were divorced. David asked for custody, but the court awarded the child to Barbara, in accordance with the general policy existing at the time. David, by then a successful ad agency executive, agreed to substantial alimony and child-support payments. He was given liberal visitation rights, and Barbara was ordered to keep the child within the Southern California area. All in all, a very ordinary situation.

Things went fairly well for about a year, with David regularly picking Wendy up at Barbara's apartment for weekend visits. Then one Saturday he arrived at the apartment and found it vacant. The building superintendent told him Barbara had said she was getting married again and was leaving the Los Angeles area. She had left no forwarding address, and the superintendent couldn't recall the name of the company that moved her things. In spite of this surreptitious departure, David expected to hear from her, if only to be told where to send the child-support payments. After some weeks of silence, however, he came to me for help.

I told him Barbara was clearly in violation of the custody order and there seemed to be no legal problem in bringing her back—if we could find her. The obvious answer was to hire private detectives, but I warned him that would be expensive.

"Don't worry about money," he said. "Just find Wendy."

The detectives we hired were competent and thorough but totally unsuccessful. A check of the moving companies and the advertising and model agencies turned up nothing. Neither did interviews with Barbara's friends and relatives. The nearest thing we had to leads came from two of her friends who said she had talked about going abroad and a relative who said Barbara had talked about getting married but hadn't given the man's name. A woman and a three-year-old child had simply vanished.

Years went by and David married again. He and his second wife had a son, but he never gave up trying to find Wendy. Periodically the detective agency was engaged to reinterview the friends and relatives. But at the end of three years it appeared we'd reached a dead end.

Then, late one night, I was awakened by the phone. "Marvin, it's me, David," an almost hysterical voice shouted. "I've found Wendy!"

David and his wife had been to see a new French movie called *Gigot,* which starred Jackie Gleason and a new child star billed as Diane Gardner. "The moment she appeared on the screen I recognized Wendy," he said excitedly. "I made so much noise they almost tossed us out of the theater."

I was a little skeptical and reminded him it had been years since he'd seen the child and that she'd been scarcely more than a baby.

"Marvin, I *know,*" he insisted. "You've got to believe me. It's Wendy!"

We contacted the American film company that made the movie, but they told us the casting had been done in France and that names and addresses of the local talent would have to be obtained there. I contacted a French lawyer with whom I had worked before and asked him to hire detectives and do whatever was necessary.

Within a week, I received a cable: CHILD WENDY DIANE WEYLAND. MOTHER MARRIED ROY E. GARDNER, ADMITS IDENTITY. DETAILS MAILED.

In no mood to wait for the mails, David came to my office and we put in a call to my Paris colleague. The French detectives had found Barbara, Wendy, and Gardner living in Paris. But Barbara had told them, "You can tell David that Wendy's staying with me and is never going back to him. There's nothing you can do about it."

After the phone call, David made no effort to hide his tears, prompted by joy and despair. "I was right, I *knew* it was Wendy," he said. "But there must be something we can do!"

I said we'd try, though I didn't think there was much hope. Child custody violations are not subject to international extradition treaties, and so long as Barbara and Wendy stayed out of California there was little that could be done.

One day when David was almost prepared to abandon the struggle, the French lawyer called to tell us that the Paris papers reported that Wendy and the Gardners were leaving for the United States to make television appearances and perhaps a new movie.

It was hard to believe, and it was only later that we found out that a French attorney had told them they wouldn't be subject to American courts because they were French residents. Not looking this gift horse in the mouth, we ordered private detectives into round-the-clock surveillance of the trio. When they left Paris, every move across the continent and the Atlantic was monitored and reported to us.

Originally, our plan called for intercepting them when they reached New York, but while David and I were still preparing for the trip East, word was received that the Gardners planned to fly on to Los Angeles with the child for a television appearance.

It was almost unbelievable. We rushed downtown to the courthouse, hoping to obtain an order granting immediate custody of the child, pending a full custody hearing. The judge agreed to issue a *writ of habeas corpus,* which would permit the sheriff to seize the child and deliver her to David. By the time we got the writ duly signed and properly executed and convinced the sheriff to serve the writ, it was almost time for the Gardners' flight to land.

Accompanied by the deputies, we made an old-time melodramatic dash—complete with sirens to clear the route—for the Los Angeles International Airport, arriving just in time to intercept the three while they were still in the terminal. When David saw Wendy, he could no longer restrain himself and rushed ahead of the deputies to greet her. Barbara's new husband moved in to block him, and there was a brief tug-of-war with the girl in between. One of the deputies scooped up the bewildered child, and after a few minutes of struggling, the second deputy managed to break up the fight and explain the legal action. Everybody moved into a nearby waiting room for a short conference, and after a few moments of discussion, David left with his daughter.

However, it was only the beginning of the struggle. A long and bitter custody battle followed, with the Gardners trying to convince the court that Wendy's best interests lay in remaining with them and continuing her movie career. David insisted the child was being deprived of a normal childhood, which he wanted to give back to her. The Gardners introduced testimony that Wendy was a "rare talent" who could make a fortune in the industry before she was ten. She was taken into the judge's chambers alone and questioned on whether she missed being an actress. She told him it was more fun to have toys and games, to go to school, and to play with her new-found half brother and his friends. When the hearing was over, the judge ruled that Wendy should remain with her father.

That should have ended the matter. But about a year later, when David's wife went to pick Wendy up after school, she was told by the other children that a man and woman had rushed from a parked car, grabbed Wendy, and fled with her. Once again David sent the detectives out to track down leads and publicly offered a reward for information leading to the little girl's whereabouts. Once again his efforts yielded nothing but frustration and silence. And this time the silence lasted five years. At Christmas time that fifth year, Wendy sent a card, postmarked Chicago, with the message, "I'm well and send my love to all of you."

Similar cards and messages arrived for another five Christmases, each postmarked from a different city and each proving to be another dead end for the detectives David sent in cold pursuit. Then, one evening, David's doorbell rang. When he opened the door a young woman flung her arms around him and cried, "Daddy, I'm home!" Wendy was at last eighteen, able to make her own decisions, and she had made her way back to the place she had always regarded as home.

Custody fights, at best, are traumatic for both child and parents, but when legal anomalies permit an emotional parent to nullify the impartial judgment of a court, the damage done to all parties would seem to justify drastic reform of the law. At least, jurisdictional problems similar to those in the Martin and Weyland cases should be eliminated, and I have come to the conclusion that the adoption of uniform divorce and custody laws on a nationwide basis would go far toward ameliorating these situations.

CHAPTER FOURTEEN

The Child Many Fathers Share

British actress Diana Dors provided my first exposure to the reasonable way parents could, and should, respond to the child custody issue when a marriage falls apart. Diana came to the United States at the height of the Marilyn Monroe era, brought up in the net of a worldwide talent search to find a rival for the Hollywood sex goddess. Certainly she had all the physical attributes required: she was blonde, sultry, and appropriately voluptuous. Even prior to her arrival in the United States, one British newspaper had dubbed her "England's answer to Marilyn."

She and comedian Dickie Dawson had two children from their five-year marriage. Almost from the day they arrived in America, the marriage began to fall apart. Dawson was a traditional English music hall comedian, and at home his bookings were steady enough to assure a long, if not spectacular, career. In the United States, however, he found himself only an appendage to Diana. The routines that had them rolling in the aisles in London didn't mean much in Los Angeles in those days, although in later years, Dawson's humor became much more appreciated by local audiences. Diana's career, on the other hand, was on the rise, and the constant whirl of publicity sessions, meetings, and screen tests took precedence over everything. The result was a series of acrimonious quarrels between the two, and finally Diana decided to seek a divorce.

On the basis of Diana's story, therefore, I began preparing a divorce petition charging Dickie with mental and the standard cruelty. It was, in almost every sense, a rather routine action until I asked Diana what she wanted to do about Dickie's visitation rights.

"He won't need any," she answered. "I've decided to give him custody."

That was a bit of a shock. Although many women make this choice today, in the early sixties it was almost unprecedented for a mother to give up her young children voluntarily.

"Have you really thought this out?" I persisted. "Are you sure that's what you want?"

"Oh, yes," she replied without hesitation. "I have commitments to appear in pictures that are going to be filmed in locations all over the world, so it wouldn't be good for the children to take them with me. I wouldn't be able to take proper care of them. You know how it is on location—I'd be working all day, and sometimes at night. The children would be spending all their time with a nurse or housekeeper."

"I can see your point," I said. "But it is quite unusual."

"So some of my friends have already told me. They seem to think I'm some kind of unnatural mother. But I am really thinking of what's best for the children."

She looked at me seriously. "I do love them and wish I could have them with me all the time. But I'm an actress, too, and want to keep my career going. That's what's forcing me into making this kind of decision. I truly think the children will be better off with Dickie, who's a devoted father." And when finally divorced, Diana, true to her convictions, allowed Dickie to retain physical custody of the children.

Tony Curtis may have used the same kind of reasoning when he left his children with their mothers at the time his first two marriages fell apart during the most active phase of his film career. But this was never considered unusual for a man. However, it was quite unusual when, several years later, he set out to gather the children from all his broken marriages under one roof.

All I really knew about Tony before I met him was his tendency to marry beautiful women and to produce children. His first wife was actress Janet Leigh; the second, German actress Christine Kaufman; and his current one, top fashion model Leslie Meredith Allen. He had two children by each of them.

Having heard many stories about Tony over the years, I was totally unprepared for his warm and really friendly personality when I first met him at a house party he and Leslie gave at their home in London. I had been invited to the party by Seymour Lazar, a friend and brilliant financier, and went expecting it to be a sort of "old home week" with a lot of entertainment-world guests I'd probably know who would only want to talk about their next picture or last picture. Instead, I found myself among a small group of creative and professional people whose interests were in human beings and in world events of real importance.

The Curtises, realizing I was a stranger, went out of their way to make me feel at ease. When Tony noticed me admiring one of his paintings, he asked if I was interested in art, and then wanted to know about my modest collection, rather than talk about his own much more extensive one.

During our conversation, he told me, "Actually, I guess I know more about lawyers than art. But then I've had more experience with them, and they've cost me a lot more, if you include all the alimony and custody payments I'm making." Later, as I was leaving, he said, "When I get back to California, I may call you."

His call came only a few days later, however, while I was still in Europe. His problem mainly concerned custody of Allegra and Alexandra, his six- and eight-year-old daughters by Christine. Tony claimed Christine had been using the two girls as a weapon, extracting extra money from him in exchange for their visits to him. He detected what he considered signs of neglect when the girls were sent to him in London and that was what had caused him to call me so suddenly. Since Kelly, his daughter by Janet, had also expressed a desire to live with him, he thought he should attend to both custody proceedings at once.

After some discussion, we decided to wait until everyone was back in California, where the original divorces and custody orders were granted. Allegra and Alexandra were with him in London and were scheduled to return with him to Los Angeles for a summer visit. However, the children were legally domiciled in Germany, where Christine had returned after the divorce—though one of Tony's complaints was the fact that she had been traveling rather constantly about Europe with the girls, thus depriving them of environmental stability. I had never handled a double-barreled custody action, but when the Curtis family returned home some-time later, I was ready.

I didn't anticipate much of a problem with the Leigh daughters. Under California's liberalized custody code, the courts are required to consider the preferences of children who are old enough to make valid judgments. At that time, Jamie was fifteen and Kelly, at seventeen, was only a year away from the day when she would have the right to live where she chose anyway.

A review of the case file and custody agreements showed that the biggest problem was that there were no apparent grounds for changing custody of Christine's daughters, though there was evidence to back up Tony's claim that Christine had made visitations difficult on occasion. More evidence would be needed to convince the court, despite the fact that his current wife, Leslie, was as devoted to the other children as she was to her own or that he had a home big enough for all of them. Moreover, I didn't expect Christine to give the children up without a fight.

"I'd hate to do it in public," Tony said, "but if we have to, I think we can prove Christine's lifestyle is harmful to the girls. She's off traveling around so much and she leaves them with strangers a lot. Even when she's home, her private life is just a little bit too irregular."

I warned him there would be a lot of publicity if he went through with it, since I couldn't think of a situation where anyone had sued two ex-wives simultaneously before, and I anticipated that Christine would try to create an international incident out of any attempt to take the girls from her. But Tony decided that obtaining custody of the girls was more important than what anyone wrote about him, and so we went forward.

It was one of those situations where timing was extremely important. The visitation period for Allegra and Alexandra at the Curtises was about to end, so I went into court for a temporary custody order. I wanted to be sure we didn't start the main custody battle with the disadvantage of being in violation of the custody agreement for not sending them back to Germany.

Christine reacted as we expected by immediately calling a European press conference to accuse Tony of "kidnapping" the girls for the sole purpose of avoiding child-support payments. At every stop along the way, as she traveled from Germany to the United States to fight our suit, she repeated the charge and added that filing the suit in California was an insult to the German courts and the German concept of justice. (Actually, since a Los Angeles court had made the custody agreement binding in the first place and had continuing jurisdiction over the Curtis girls, we dismissed that concept out of hand.)

Once Christine arrived in Los Angeles, I warned Tony and Leslie not to allow the girls out of their sight. I wanted no repetition of any transoceanic child-grab caper. Until Christine retained local counsel and responded to our petition, I thought the danger was real, though remote.

We had obtained a number of affidavits and declarations concerning Christine's personal life and the way Allegra and Alexandra were cared for when in her custody. I considered them rather heavy ammunition and told her attorneys we'd use them all if it became necessary to attack her fitness as a mother. Apparently they agreed, for they convinced Christine to relinquish custody in return for certain modifications in her financial settlement with Tony.

This permitted us to go before a judge and ask that the new agreement be approved for "the best interests" of the children. Our main points were Tony's more settled life and the care of two parents in a home situation with other children. The anticipated hard battle, it appeared, had been resolved almost without a shot being fired.

It was Janet Leigh, however, who turned out to be our stumbling block. She was willing to acquiesce on Kelly, who was spending most of her time with Tony anyway, but she drew the line at giving up Jamie. An attempt to negotiate some kind of agreement with her failed, and after a few months of motion and countermotion in the courts, Tony decided to drop the issue.

"It's hard on Janet, and it's hard on me," he said. "But it's hardest on Jamie, and the longer we fight over her, the worse it's going to get."

In this instance, also, the "best interests" of the child were decided without having a judge determine them.

Making the true best interests of the child the paramount consideration for custody is one of the improved aspects of California's 1970 Family Law Act and is illustrative of a refreshing trend in domestic relations law everywhere today. Perhaps the Mickey Rooney case provides one of the best examples of this enlightened attitude by the courts on the issue of child custody.

I represented Don and Helen Thomason, the maternal grandparents of Rooney's four children by his fourth wife. While her divorce from Rooney was still pending, Barbara Thomason Rooney was killed by Yugoslavian actor Milos Milosevic, who then turned the gun on himself. For the next six years the children lived with the Thomasons, who were named co-guardians with Rooney after the shooting.

The custody arrangement was an informal one and Rooney, who went through a series of quick marriages and quicker divorces, was married to his seventh wife, Carolyn, and was talking about taking his children back. The pair were living in Florida, and Rooney had adopted his new wife's seven-year-old son by a previous marriage.

For six years while Rooney struggled with career and personal problems, the grandparents had devoted their lives to their dead daughter's children. His visits were sporadic and infrequent, and he contributed little to their support. Meanwhile, the Thomasons and the children had become so attached to each other that the older couple were loath to give them up. Now they became concerned that Rooney would simply come and take them away. Their concern gave way to reality when Rooney filed a formal motion to do just that.

The Thomasons asked me to represent them in their counterbid to retain physical custody. I did not know them, but Helen Thomason said they sought me out at first because before the murder Barbara had told her she planned to retain me in her divorce action.

The case posed some interesting challenges, not the least of which was an apparent conflict between the Probate Code's standard for granting child guardianships and the 1970 Family Law Act's prerequisite for making a child custody award. While the two California statutes were not in direct conflict, they left a shadow in the field of judicial discretion.

"In appointing a general guardian of a minor," Probate Code Section 1406 states, "the court is to be guided by what appears to be for the best interest of the child in respect to its temporal and mental and moral welfare...."

But according to Civil Code Section 4600 (which contains the Family Law Act),

... before the Court makes any order awarding custody to a person or persons other than the parent, without consent of the parents, it must make a finding that an award of custody to a parent would be detrimental to the child, and the award to a nonparent is required to serve the best interests of the child....

While the "best interests" doctrine is explicitly mentioned in both code sections, the latter implies a necessity to *prove actual harm* to the child before the parent can be refused custody. The statute carefully avoids using the term "unfitness," but it was obvious we'd have to prove something quite close to that before we could prevent Rooney from regaining custody. It was a double burden on us, since all Rooney apparently needed to prove was that it wouldn't harm the children for him to have them.

Helen Thomason's willingness to raise a second family in the face of tragedy turned me from a mere legal advocate to a defender of a cause, the one thing a lawyer should avoid doing lest he lose his sense of objectivity. I badly wanted to win. The trial itself also provided one of the few opportunities in my whole career to play a Perry Mason-like role in the courtroom, with eleventh-hour evidence leading to the dramatic "breaking" of a key witness on cross-examination.

We put on a strong case, proving that the children's "temporal and mental and moral" best interests had so far been served in the Thomason home and called a number of witnesses to show this, including a psychiatrist who testified that the children were "well-adjusted, happy, and content." We also produced a Superior Court judge who had known the Thomasons for many years. He declared that the children were "very, very fortunate" to be in the Thomasons' custody, and added, "I wish my children had been raised as well as these children are being raised."

Rooney's past record of neglect was illustrated by a diary Mrs. Thomason had begun keeping when the children first came to live with her. It showed a long record of infrequent visits, broken promises, forgotten birthdays, and failure to even write to the children. One portion pertained to a time when Rooney stayed in Los Angeles for an extended period, making almost daily visits to the race track—but none to his children living only a few blocks away.

We were faced with weakness of evidence based on recent behavior, and Rooney set out to build a strong case on the parental preference rule and the fact that any demonstrable "unfitness" was something from the past.

On the witness stand he was humble, contrite, and conciliatory. He painted a picture of himself as a changed man who could now offer his children "a whole new life." The change was credited to religious conversion and to his new wife, Carolyn, a statuesque blonde twenty years younger than he.

She made a great witness for Rooney, perhaps more so because she flew in from Florida at the last minute, giving me no opportunity to examine her in a pretrial deposition. In her testimony she came across as something between a saint and the original Earth Mother. She "loved children," she said, and she "loved Mickey's children." They called her "Mother" when visiting in Florida. There was no question that she could "take care" of the four of them plus her child from her first marriage. That marriage had been "a tragic mistake." True, her first husband had filed for the divorce—but that was only because her religion "forbade divorce."

She was simply too good to be true. During cross-examination, she maintained she "couldn't remember" the grounds for the divorce, and that her former husband had no objections to Rooney adopting his child. "He had no interest in the baby," she said. "It was just something in a crib to him." Somehow, she seemed to me, too much like a real live female version of Mr. Clean. "My God," I thought, "this is the nicest woman I've ever seen." That led me to ask as my next question, "Were you granted custody at the time of the divorce?"

She hesitated for just an instant—long enough, however, for the judge to uphold her attorney's objection that the question was collateral to the main issue. I felt I was onto something but was prevented from further inquiry by the lawyer's objecting to my inquiring into the first marriage. About the only other thing I was permitted to find out was the name of her former husband and the fact that he lived in Columbus, Ohio.

Testimony was virtually completed by the weekend recess, and I felt the judgment was still in doubt—with the law guaranteeing Rooney the benefit of that doubt. On a hunch, I decided to play weekend detective. From the information operator I obtained a list of telephone numbers of persons with her husband's last name who were living in Columbus and started calling them one by one until I found her former husband.

The information he provided was a bombshell, but not totally unexpected. Their divorce, it seems, had been granted on grounds of gross neglect and filed, not for religious reasons, but because Carolyn had deserted him and their child—leaving a note in which she said that she didn't want the child. Later, she wrote a long confessional letter stating she had been wrong. She told him she had gotten psychiatric help and was now married to Rooney, who wanted to adopt the baby. The ex-husband, a construction worker, said it was hard for him to work and care for the child as well, and figuring Rooney had money to provide a better future for the boy, had allowed Carolyn to regain custody. He also said her "confession" letter and other documentary proof were available but that he couldn't afford to leave his job to testify in California.

Lacking a Paul Drake on my staff, I was forced to send my law clerk, Bob Ross, on overnight cross-country flights to round up the evidence. It went off, in true Perry Mason style. Bob located the original divorce lawyer, now a judge, who was then off fishing in Michigan. Then he looked up his brother, who had taken over the practice and had the records—and who for a long time couldn't find them. Then Bob's return flight was cancelled, forcing me to use up Monday morning in court stalling for time, until the afternoon session.

But the documents, including the damning letter, arrived just in time to call Carolyn as my final rebuttal witness. There was intense objection to the introduction of the new evidence at such a late stage. Rooney's lawyer barely had time to tell Carolyn that I was out to destroy her earlier testimony before she took the stand. The strain was obvious in her face, and when Carolyn realized I knew the real facts of her first marriage, the little remaining composure she'd been able to muster vanished.

I took no pleasure from the questioning that slowly undermined her testimony, making me realize I wouldn't care for the Perry Mason routine as a steady diet. When I started reading from the confessional letter, Carolyn broke down completely and Rooney rushed from the counsel table to take her in his arms. As he passed me, he snarled an almost old-fashioned word, "Cur!"

Custody was awarded to the Thomasons by Judge Mario Clinco who stated he hoped the decision would be appealed to clarify the law. It wasn't. And Rooney's seventh marriage has since disintegrated, proving in my mind, at least, that the children's best interests were in fact served by the court's decision.

In the Dors, Curtis, and Rooney cases the ultimate custody determination did indeed work out to the best interests of the children, from Diana's decision not to attempt to do what would have been a job of child raising that would have been unfair to her children, to Tony's crusade to "keep it all in the family," to Judge Clinco's innovative interpretation of a new statute and awarding the children to nonparents rather than a natural parent. However, children will probably always be the innocent victims of marital breakups, and I often wonder if a special custody court couldn't be established to help protect their interests. It could be a court in which lawyers played no part, a court made up of a judge or commissioner, aided by a psychiatrist or psychologist and a sociologist—a court where not the letter of the law but solely the best interests of the children would be the sole consideration in determining their custody.

CHAPTER FIFTEEN

It's a Wise Child

Paternity is one issue lawyers are dealing with less frequently than they were a few decades ago. The decline in litigation is primarily the result of changing social attitudes that have virtually removed the stigma of bastardy from a child, and rather than total social condemnation, the unwed mother now is viewed more with softened disapproval.

For instance, shortly after World War II, the disclosure that actress Ingrid Bergman was bearing Italian director Roberto Rosselini's child created an international scandal, provoking one U.S. senator to call Hollywood a modern Sodom and Gomorrah and branding Miss Bergman's behavior a "stain on the nation's character." But public attitudes have changed so much that a child born to a public figure today hardly raises anyone's eyebrow. The roster of bachelor parents is longer than the Academy Award nomination list and includes some of the same names. Yet, whatever the activities of the famous, they represent only the tip of the iceberg: one recent study of children born to women under twenty in the United States indicated that more than 25 percent were conceived out of wedlock.

The decline in paternity suits is also one of the outcomes of the social and economic "liberation" of women. Many women no longer marry their "love child's" father, since it is no longer necessary for their social or financial survival. "Why should I marry the no good son of a bitch?" one woman told me recently. "I don't want my baby to have a father like that." Of course, birth-control pills and other widely disseminated forms of contraception, plus liberalized abortion laws in many states, have combined to prevent a number of paternity suits from coming into. existence in the first place.

Like divorce laws, paternity laws are also made by the individual states, and most of them automatically require that the man support his offspring once he is ruled to be the father. Among the paternity suits I have handled in my practice over the years, some involved bizarre legal tangles and some involved the classic way that created so many Hollywood paternity scandals in the pre-World War II era.

A case that developed along these latter lines involved rock music star Stephen Stills, at that time a member of The Buffalo Springfield, one of the top rock groups. Harriet, a dark-haired Pennsylvania farm girl had come to Hollywood, not in search of the traditional movie stardom but to be part of the rock music scene. On the surface she was a product of the rock subculture, dressing the part, speaking the jargon, giving the impression of being a "chick who knew the score," but that was apparently as far as it went. She loved the music and went along with the unconventional conduct of the rock world, but her own strict upbringing held her to a different set of values. So, while she tolerated those who used drugs and slept around, she herself did not touch drugs or "smoke grass" and spent her nights alone in her own bed.

She was a secretary at one of the recording studios when she met Stills at a Beverly Hills nightclub opening of his musical group. It wasn't exactly love at first sight. As she ultimately testified before the jury, when he stopped by the table where she sat with friends during a break in the performance, his first words were, "I think you and I can make it." She laughed off that first remark. But, later, when he pressed her for a date, she told him that if he was looking for sex he was making a mistake; she was a virgin who intended to stay one until marriage.

Stills apparently took the warning and its later reiteration as a personal challenge. "No" seems to be a word that rock superstars seldom hear when they try to take up with one of the "groupies" who follow them around. For two years Stills pursued to conquer. The pursuit was rather desultory; there were, after all, plenty of others who had no qualms. He didn't work very hard or very often at seeing Harriet, but he did keep coming around. And after a while, she fell in love with him.

"At first, he was always kind and gentle," she testified, "and sort of exciting to be with, although he never let me forget what he was after, and he was always on the make." She'd been outtalking or outrunning men since she was fourteen but being in love made it harder to say no, especially when Stills kept reminding her of something she knew too well. There were plenty of girls hanging around who wouldn't and didn't say no to anything. Eventually, he beat down her defense and in 1968 they started an affair.

The relationship ended exactly as Harriet's mother or Ann Landers might have predicted; with the sexual conquest complete, Stills rapidly lost interest. She gave him a gold key to her apartment, but they never really lived together. He was away on concerts and appearances and, of course, he had other girls, and other apartments.

In the spring of 1969 Harriet became pregnant. Stills later claimed he intended to end the relationship long before he learned she was pregnant, and he also denied being with Harriet that week of the baby's conception. His lawyers made a number of offers, involving both lump-sum payments and trust funds for the child, provided she withdraw the paternity charge. She was determined, however, that her son have a legal father. When I entered the case, the child was almost two years old, and Harriet was still insisting Stills was the only man she had ever slept with, and whatever the cost, the rock star's recognition of their son was more important to her than any amount of money offered in settlement.

After a lengthy negotiation with Stills' attorneys, I told Harriet the court might award less money than she'd been offered, even if a jury decided Stills was the father. I also felt it necessary to point out that we could even lose if the case went to trial. I tried to explain that every jury trial is a gamble because the jurors must decide factual issues largely on the basis of what they are told in the courtroom—and it would be simply her word against Stills' that he was the father. "We *can't* lose," she insisted, "because Stephen *is* the father!" To her, the issue was as self-evident as the sunrise.

The facts in a lawsuit are supposed to be established by the preponderance of the evidence and the credibility of the witnesses, but it is a Solomonic task, even for judges trained in the rules of law and in the rhetoric of logical discourse. No better safeguard for justice has yet been devised than the jury system, yet it would be unrealistic to ignore the fact that people tend to make judgments based on personal experience, convictions, and beliefs. The legal system itself recognizes this human failing by providing for *voir dire,* the preselection questioning of prospective jurors to unearth hidden prejudices and attitudes that might cloud their judgment in a given case. In jurisdictions where liberal *voir dire* is permitted, jury selection is often the most crucial point of the trial.

A great deal of time was spent by both sides in selecting jurors for the Stills paternity trial, even though questioning of jurors was conducted by the judge under the new judicial rules in this regard. I sought to avoid empaneling a jury of young, single men or so-called swingers (who might envision themselves as future defendants in a paternity action) and people with puritanical religious views (who might adopt a punitive attitude toward Harriet). The ideal jury, from my point of view, would have been twelve married women who could sympathize with Harriet's plight and who had teen-aged daughters capable of becoming involved in similar romantic indiscretions. Stills' lawyers naturally were interested in keeping such jurors off the panel, and since both sides had a limited number of jury challenges, we ended up with something of a compromise. The jury finally selected was composed of eight women and four men. Five were middle-aged mothers; the others were young women whom I hoped could imagine themselves in similar predicaments. The men were mainly of a conventional or conservative nature, and I hoped they'd be more "turned off" by the lifestyle of Stills and his friends than by Harriet's "fallen woman" status.

It was the kind of case where the jury's evaluation of the witnesses and their credibility would be crucial. We had blood tests made, of course, but such tests only show that a man of that blood type could or could not be the father; yet, science has devised no way of proving that a specific person actually *is* the father. We also had Stills' admission that he had been intimate with Harriet over a period of time. Beyond this, however, there was no point of agreement.

Stills' main defense was that he had not been with Harriet or been intimate with her during the week that medical evidence had established the child was conceived. A number of alibi witnesses, which included members of his band, testified in an effort to refute Harriet's story of sexual intimacy during that week. The defense even presented a "girl friend" who claimed she had had sexual relations with Stills the very night that Harriet claimed to have rendezvoused with Stephen. Such testimony is typical of the classic paternity defense, both to confuse the issue of possible fathers and to impugn the woman's assertion that she had had no other sexual contact.

Stills' lawyers tried to show that it was impossible for him to be the father, because during the crucial few days when conception was possible he was either in Hawaii in a recording studio with the band or in bed with another woman. The first defense was made less believable when we produced business and travel records to prove he had returned from Hawaii in plenty of time to be the baby's father. His claim of being in a recording studio was undermined when we pointed out the reason for his Hawaiian trip: he had broken his hand; it was in a cast, and he couldn't play his guitar with any great facility. The "other woman" defense was significantly weakened when their witness admitted on the stand that she hadn't been with Stills all of the time on either of the nights in question. In fact, she testified that on one of the nights she expected him by 10:00 P.M., and he showed up closer to 4:00 in the morning—some six hours later. The other man that Stills' lawyers contended might be the father was eliminated by blood tests showing that scientifically he couldn't be the father.

Thus, the main problem before the jury became one of deciding which story made the most sense and whose witnesses were the more believable. Stills' broken hand and the heavy cast around it played an important role in attacking the credibility of his fellow musicians and their detailed, if contradictory, recollections about the recording sessions. The two days in question had occurred more than three years before, and it would be expected that the musicians, with their particular lifestyle, would have difficulty remembering even what they had for breakfast that morning. But their memories about those two isolated days were almost perfect—except that one recalled that the cast was off and another wasn't sure. Everyone insisted Stills had participated in the recording sessions, though that seemed hard to believe because it was held only two weeks after the hand was broken—regardless of whether a cast was on it or not. One musician testified how well Stills had played and said he particularly remembered because they were recording one of their biggest hit records, a song called "Deja Vu." This remarkable recollection was, no doubt, diminished somewhat in the jury's estimation when we introduced evidence showing "Deja Vu" had been recorded and released a year *before* the baby was conceived.

Harriet told her story of one-sided love in a simple, straightforward, poignant, and sometimes tearful, manner. It was obvious she had been, and probably still was, deeply in love, whereas the rock star plainly considered her first a challenge and later a troublesome problem. However, the child himself turned out to be the best witness in the whole trial, for he bore a striking resemblance to Stills. Since it's permissible in paternity trials to use the child as evidence, I paraded the two-year-old past the jury, with the musician following close behind, so the jurors could note the resemblance, or lack of it. Stills had pointedly ignored the child throughout the trial but, for some reason, he chose one moment to bend a little. He smiled and cocked a finger at the happy youngster. The boy grinned and pointed back with his tiny forefinger. "Da-da!" he said, to the surprised jurors, amid an outburst of heartwarming courtroom laughter.

The jury verdict was unanimous, but Harriet's court award, as I had feared, was significantly less in monetary terms than Stills' lawyers had offered for out-of-court settlement. It didn't matter to her. As we left the court, someone murmured, "Congratulations." She turned to smile and said, "Stephen is the one who should be congratulated. He's just won a beautiful son." Indeed he had—the hard way.

My first exposure to the so-called "nonpaternity" case, a rarity in itself, came as a double one at that. One client's former husband sued to have himself declared not to be the father, while the former husband of another client sued to assert that he was indeed the father of my client's son, as opposed to the claims of her present husband—a sort of reverse nonpaternity.

Academy Award winning actor Gig Young filed a suit in an attempt to be relieved of medical costs and child-support payments several years after he and his wife Elaine (my client) were divorced. The grounds cited for the 1970 legal action were a vasectomy in 1938, which he claimed made it impossible for him to father any child, and included an accusation that Elaine had deceived him into believing he had fathered the child because some kind of "medical miracle" had occurred. Scientifically, his position may have had merit, but from a human standpoint it was pretty thin. He had always recognized the child before the divorce and, indeed, had been very devoted to her. He hadn't opposed the divorce petition and moreover had signed a property settlement wherein he acknowledged the child as his own. In fact, one of the things that led to the lawsuit was Elaine's petition for extra child-support money to pay for psychiatric treatment of the child's severe insecurity problems stemming from the girl's loss of a relationship with her father.

I was reasonably certain the little girl would get her father back as a matter of law, in spite of the factual situation Gig and his lawyers were trying to create. I was equally hopeful it could be done without the necessity of a long jury trial and the embarrassing public exposure that would be sure to follow.

California law presumes the husband of a married woman is the father of any child she bears, and we contended the time had long passed when Young could properly question it. To forestall the

-145-

threatened public spectacle, I filed for a summary judgment based on the legal questions of *res judicata* and *laches*. A summary judgment is one granted by the court without trial on the issues of the factual situation or the materiality of the evidence. *Res judicata* is a legal term that means, literally, the issue has already been decided; *laches* means the complainant waited an unreasonable length of time to seek a remedy at law, a type of equitable statute of limitations.

We contended that any question of paternity was settled by the court in the divorce decree ruling and that the only issue properly before it concerned the child-support payments. I also argued that the principle of *laches* applied, because Young had ample opportunity to raise the paternity question, both when the child was born and at the time of the divorce. The judge agreed, and his judgment was ultimately upheld by the District Court of Appeals and then the California Supreme Court.

Paternity suits seem almost like custody cases in reverse, where one party is trying to make the other accept the child or, in some cases, deny the other party's right to the child. It is one of the more unpleasant aspects of domestic relations law, because of the damage necessarily done to the children who may end up without fathers, or even sadder, become aware that their fathers really don't want to recognize them. Yet, so long as the marriage institution survives in its present form, paternity suits will most likely remain a necessary evil.

CHAPTER SIXTEEN

Let No Man Put Asunder

In the United States, marriage and divorce are civil rather than religious matters. The Constitutional separation of church and state means that the institution of marriage is under the legal control of secular authorities. However, social custom and tradition often create anomalies: most states will recognize the validity of a *religious marriage,* even if a couple fails to obtain a license at City Hall first; but no state recognizes a *religious divorce*—indeed, it has no force in law at all.

The influence of religion goes far beyond the marriage ceremony, and sometimes it crops up in a divorce proceeding in a way that is completely inappropriate. Attempts are sometimes made to force religious tenets into divorce actions where one party neither shares nor understands them. Such a move was made by actress Terry Moore, one-time girlfriend of Howard Hughes, in her divorce from stockbroker Stuart Cramer III, scion of an old Southern family, who himself was formerly married to Jean Peters, who later became Hughes' second wife.

Stuart was my client, and Terry was represented by Robert Neeb, who had been an associate of the late Jerry Geisler, the one-time famed celebrity divorce lawyer. Neeb had established a rather formidable reputation in his own right, especially in the area of community property settlements. He had earned the local record for such settlements by uncovering more than $16 million worth of hidden assets belonging to the spouse of a lady divorce client whom several prominent lawyers had declined to represent.

The fact that Neeb had engaged in limited pretrial discovery in our case disturbed me. I was certain he had some kind of legal ace up his sleeve, but I couldn't figure out what it was.

Much of Stuart's wealth had been inherited from his family before the marriage, and we had ample documentary proof that these assets hadn't been co-mingled with his business operations at any time during the marriage. To my way of thinking, they remained his own separate property and were not subject to division under the community property laws. But Terry was claiming half on the theory of oral transmutation, or the contention that he had, by word of mouth, made her a gift of the property he acquired before their marriage.

It wasn't until the day we were scheduled to start the divorce trial that I discovered the basis for Terry's exorbitant community property claims. She and Neeb showed up at the Santa Monica courthouse with a couple of men among their witness group who obviously were some sort of church officials. I jokingly asked Neeb if he planned to have the church testify against my client. Very seriously, he suggested we discuss it outside the court.

"You have a problem with the so-called separate property," he told me as we walked along in the morning sunlight, "because your client agreed to share it with Terry at their wedding."

"He did?" I asked with a disbelief that was only half-feigned. Stuart had gone out of his way, in my opinion, to be more than fair in his attitude toward Terry and the settlement of their divorce problems. It seemed unlikely he would not have mentioned such an agreement, considering her claims against him.

Neeb grinned knowingly. "Terry's a Mormon you know, and they were married in a Mormon ceremony." I must have shown my bafflement, for his grin became wider. "In Mormon marriage vows," he said, "the couple agree to *share everything,* both in this life and the next."

It was a novel way to support an oral transmutation contention, but I was certain it had neither legal precedent nor legal force. I told Neeb he had an interesting and ingenious argument, though I remained confident the case would be decided on the basis of California statutes, not on the basis of the *Book of Mormon.* The issue, as well as the fact that he intended to put some Mormon church elders on the witness stand to explain it, left me uncomfortable, however. Oral transmutation is always a tenuous argument, though frequently used by many lawyers when there isn't any other way of demonstrating a valid claim to marriage assets. I didn't think Neeb's point about marriage vows was a very good one, and I didn't think the court would buy it, but in a trial you can't be sure of anything.

While waiting for the judge to finish a trial scheduled ahead of us, I questioned Stuart about the wedding. He had, indeed, gone through a Mormon ceremony, but he hadn't considered it a significant thing—just something Terry and her family wanted but that didn't really make any difference to him. He was not a Mormon then and hadn't become since, and he thought Neeb's contention preposterous. I knew little about the Mormon faith, but I was sure Stuart's nonmember status would be a good defense against any argument that the marriage vows had established an obligation to share his separate property.

With Neeb's permission, I questioned the elders about the tenets of the Mormon religion and the requirements for conversion to the faith. Marriage with non-Mormons was permitted by their church, they confirmed, but such marriages did not automatically confer Mormon status on the outsider. Conversion required a different ritual, after a thorough study of the religion's basic doctrines.

After hearing this explanation, the wedding vow, oral transmutation theory seemed quite weak to me, and I told Neeb as much. We went for another walk outside to discuss it because I noticed the elders were taking my legal questioning as a personal attack on their religion.

"Look, Bob," I said, "Stuart wants to be fair, but I couldn't let him make a settlement based on the *Book of Mormon* even if he wanted to, and he doesn't." I added that as much as I admired his ingenuity in bringing up such an interesting theory, I was certain it wouldn't stand up in court. We both agreed to talk with our clients some more to try to work out an agreeable settlement before starting the trial.

Stuart, wishing to avoid the exposure of a public trial, was willing to increase the amount of his settlement offer in the interests of protecting Terry and the children from further gossip or embarrassment. I went back to Neeb with the new figure, emphasizing that neither Stuart nor I believed the court would uphold the church vows.

"Stuart simply prefers not to go to court," I said, "but he isn't going to bargain either. This is the final offer."

Terry ultimately agreed to accept Stuart's offer, which eliminated the necessity of holding a trial to determine whether the formal language of a particular religious ritual should be enforced by civil court. But it posed an interesting question, though I have no doubt it would have been ultimately rejected by the court. It might also, however, have been an expensive issue to disprove if the case had gone to trial. The advantage of an out-of-court settlement is that it ends litigation immediately and decisively.

Actress Sharon Farrell came to me a few years ago with a problem that raised another facet of religious intrusion into civil legal processes. In her case, it was a question of how far from the mainstream of orthodox religion church marriages can be and still merit civil recognition. For the official doctrine of separation of church and state to hold true, a marriage ceremony performed by a far-out guru must be granted the same legal status as one performed by a priest, minister, or rabbi. However, "prevalent moral and political theories" at any given time—which Supreme Court Justice Oliver Wendell Holmes once observed "have a good deal to do in determining the rules by which men should be governed,"—also play a major part in deciding which religious figures receive secular recognition.

Sharon was a chic blonde from Iowa whose quick rise to stardom in films like *The Reivers* and *The Love Machine* was interrupted when she vanished into the White King Soap family's Kennedy-like compound in Malibu, to play "wife" of soap heir John Boyer III. It was the typical, torrid romance of society boy meeting movie star, but it had a few novel ingredients. One was that Boyer's mother and grandmother controlled the family fortune. Another was Sharon's pregnancy and the birth of a male child. The third was an unorthodox marriage ceremony, performed by a fellow actor who was an ordained minister of a religious cult.

When Sharon came to me, her relationship with Boyer had soured, and his grandmother was trying to force her out of their house in the family compound. When the couple first started living together, Boyer told his family they had eloped. The Boyer family was an old one, long established in Los Angeles society, and John's choice of a mere actress as a "wife" no doubt shook the family sense of propriety. But the older women nevertheless accepted the situation, perhaps in a desire to understand the overly informal ways of the young.

Their acceptance was important, for Boyer's income came from trust funds administered by his grandmother, who had the power to cut him off if she considered that his conduct warranted it. After Sharon's and his baby was born, Boyer began to worry that his family would discover they weren't really married. Then, during the filming of *The Love Machine,* the subject came up late one evening at an informal party at the home of actor John Philip Law. Since he was an ordained minister of the Universal Life Church, Law saw no problem in the Farrell-Boyer dilemma and agreed to marry them on the spot.

Because Law was also rather deeply involved in Eastern mysticism, Oriental religions, Indian ceremonial rites, and other esoteric philosophies, the ceremony that followed was somewhat irregular but, according to Sharon's description of it, as touching as most. He scattered some feathers about, did a Hopi Indian dance and some chanting, and everyone took some puffs on a peyote pipe that was passed ceremoniously around the circle. Then Law pronounced them man and wife.

Afterward, Sharon said she felt just as married as if the ceremony had been performed by a bishop in a cathedral. She knew nothing of the religious tenets of the Universal Life Church and said she had no reason to question Law's status as a minister. Actually, anyone could obtain ordination in that church—headquartered in central California—simply by writing to it. All that was necessary was to send a nominal sum of money and the statement that one felt a spiritual calling. The certificate of ordination would come back by return mail.

Later, when Boyer decided to end his relationship with Sharon, he told his mother and grandmother everything, including his belief that the marriage ceremony was invalid. Their family lawyers agreed, and the grandmother ordered Sharon to leave the compound. She refused and told them she considered the marriage as valid and legally binding as any other religiously performed ceremony.

"So far as I'm concerned," she told them, "I'm John's rightful wife. I've borne his child, I used my money to support this household, and the minister who married us was validly ordained."

The one thing she didn't have, of course, was a $6 civil marriage license, which would have eliminated all question of the marriage's validity. The law, however, recognizes some forms of irregular marriage, although it takes an act of the court to establish this recognition for marriages that are not in the civil registers.

My first task was to get the question before the courts, which we accomplished by filing a divorce action that also sought recognition of the marriage's validity. There was an immediate need to obtain some kind of temporary support for Sharon and her child pending full trial of the action, and for this purpose I raised the issue of a putative spousal relationship, intending to pursue the validity of Law's marriage ceremony later, when the main divorce trial began.

A "putative spouse" is the legal term used to describe a person who believes he or she is married and acts according to that belief. For the purposes of the limited hearing on temporary alimony and child support, I considered that the putative spousal relationship would be easier to establish than the marriage's validity. Boyer's attorneys naturally insisted there was no way John Law's unorthodox Indian ceremony could have been considered valid by Sharon, and they questioned her belief in the authenticity of his credentials as an ordained minister.

Thus, Sharon's belief that Law was a bona fide minister and that the marriage ceremony was a binding one became the main issue of the temporary support hearing. Under oath she repeated the same story she had related to me, and she stayed with it during cross-examination by Boyer's lawyers. They tried to question her on her knowledge of the Universal Life Church philosophy, but I blocked that with an objection on grounds that theology was not material to the hearing. The judge agreed and ruled there was sufficient evidence of a putative spousal relationship to justify awarding her almost $2,000 a month in temporary alimony and support.

The Boyer lawyers tried to raise a question of John's ability to pay, based on grounds that he had no money of his own. Technically, perhaps, they were correct. But I argued the Boyer family had given the couple money all during the time they thought he was married, sometimes as much as $3,000 a month or more, and had paid all of their bills. In addition, we charged John had spent much of the money from Sharon's film earnings to buy polo ponies and other luxuries. My contention that John had the ability to support her, whether he earned the money or received it as a gift, was accepted by the court, and the family, in effect, was ordered to pay the temporary support, providing the case with another unusual twist.

I never got the opportunity to try in court the issue of whether a Hopi ceremony performed by a mail-order minister was a legally valid religious marriage, although I considered that issue important enough to take all the way to the U.S. Supreme Court, if necessary. Sharon, however, was not interested in fighting anything to the higher courts or even battling in the lower ones, unless absolutely necessary. Eventually, my opposition to any settlement offer that didn't include recognition of the marriage—which I considered a vital legal point for her own protection—caused her to feel it might be better to change lawyers. I agreed, and with new attorneys, a settlement was reached.

The Cramer and Farrell cases are examples of what can happen when extra-legal influences of religion are interjected in civil legal processes. Although neither case went to trial, both illustrate the difficulties inherent in the religious underpinnings of the conventional institution of marriage. If there were (as it was when religion gained control over marriage in medieval times) only one ecclesiastical authority and one faith, such religious influence would be, perhaps, harmless. But with a nation like ours, with many different religions and faiths, legal intervention to determine validity of marriage remains a distinct possibility.

Because there is no state church and no state-sanctioned official doctrine, religious intrusion into the civil process is apt to be decidedly unfair to at least one party. Terry Moore may well have believed the wedding vows entitled her to a full share of Stuart's worldly goods, but he obviously knew nothing about such a commitment. Sharon Farrell believed her Hopi wedding was valid; John Boyer felt it wasn't. In either case, once the ceremony was performed there was no way to undo the harm, and one of the parties in each action was bound to feel somewhat betrayed by the system.

CHAPTER SEVENTEEN

The End of the Affair

It isn't just marriage ceremonies, legal or otherwise, that produce feelings of betrayal. Vows, promises, gifts freely given in anticipation of marriage and then withdrawn, have also led to courtroom drama. In fact, there was a time when the country was almost inundated by breach of promise lawsuits filed by young women who felt they had been deceived into giving up their chastity on the promise of a marriage license that never materialized. They subsequently found themselves jilted somewhere between the premarital bed and the altar. So many of these outraged women sought revenge from the courts that most states, California included, eventually decided to apply the principle of *caveat emptor* (let the buyer beware) to the rules of courtship.

The breach of promise laws and another "heart balm" statute called alienation of affections had been repealed in California long before I started practicing law. However, in the winter of 1971 I became involved in international cause celebre which came close to the classic breach of promise action, only in reverse. My client was a Bel-Air multimillionaire named Ralph Stolkin who felt he had been duped and jilted by an English society beauty. The litigation was filed in the London High Court through the offices of my associate David Jacobs, so my official role was that of Stolkin's American legal advisor.

As with most disputes where money and power are involved, there were some real questions about who had jilted whom and who was most guilty of acting in bad faith. But the real issue before the court was something more tangible: the exact nature of more than $600,000 worth of "love gifts" Stolkin had lavishly bestowed on dark-haired Patricia Rawlings Wolfson during an eight-month transcontinental romance.

Ralph Stolkin was an "Horatio Alger" type character who parlayed a modest Chicago mail-order business into an oil-rich investment fortune once estimated at more than $100 million. At the age of thirty-four, he was named president of RKO Radio Pictures for a brief period after Howard Hughes sold the movie production firm in 1952 for more than $7 million. But a year after his whirlwind romance with the English beauty, Stolkin filed a Chapter 11 bankruptcy. By the time the "love gifts" lawsuit went on trial in London, however, Ralph had paid his creditors off in full and become financially successful again with a net worth still in the millions.

Patricia Wolfson had been in European high society all her life and had a special kind of "class" which often makes self-made men fall head over heels in love. She also had beauty. Her bewitching dark and sultry looks served as the model for Pietro Annigoni's Royal Academy of Arts portrait of "The Witch." Her debutante coming-out party at eighteen was held at Claridge's, to which society figures from all over Europe came to drink and toast the new belle at three separate bars in a lavish reproduction fashioned after New York's El Morocco nightclub. In the social whirl that followed, Patricia Rawlings became a frequent companion of the Aga Khan and was often seen dancing until the small hours in the fashionable bistros of Paris, London, and Rome.

Still in the social whirl at age twenty-one, Patricia turned up as guest of the Duke of Norfolk at Arundel Castle at the same time Queen Elizabeth and Prince Philip were there for the Goodwood races. Two years later she married David Wolfson, nephew of textile magnate Sir Isaac Wolfson, a neighbor in Grosvenor Square whom she'd known most of her life. Within seven months the newlyweds were vacationing separately on the French Riviera. By the middle of 1966, there was no doubt that the separation was complete.

That same summer at St. Tropez, Patricia met Ralph and began seeing him almost daily, becoming a frequent guest on his million-dollar yacht purchased from cosmetics king Charles Revlon. Ralph was fifty-three at the time. His long marriage to Ruth Koolish was over in fact, if not legally. The year before, in the wake of the break up, he went to Europe for the first time to explore new lifestyles for himself. Although when I first met Ralph, I found him to be a somewhat reticent and socially shy financial wizard, his activities and involvements in European society led the British press to describe him as a jet-set playboy.

When Stolkin returned to the United States, he arranged to meet Patricia in New York. After three days on the East Coast, they flew to his Palm Springs home in California. She later said that it was in Palm Springs that "I fell in love with Ralph, and I think he did with me."

Before she returned to London in the fall, Patricia told Ralph she would try to obtain a quick divorce from Wolfson, so she could be free to marry again. She later claimed that while she knew Stolkin had been married and had children, she thought he had been divorced when she met him.

After a month's stay in England, Patricia returned to Palm Springs with her mother to show Mrs. Rawlings how very happy she was with Ralph, and that she "wouldn't be making another mistake if we married." Within a few hours after they arrived in Palm Springs, Stolkin gave Patricia a pair of diamond and emerald bracelets, and a few days later made a formal proposal which she accepted after talking it over with her mother. The trio went to New York to celebrate the engagement, where Stolkin bought a 14-carat diamond engagement ring worth $167,000.

For several months, Stolkin lived up to the jet-setter label given him by the British press, following Patricia around the international party circuits of London, Paris, and Rome, with occasional side trips to New York and Palm Springs.

While in Paris one week, the couple went window-shopping at Cartier's. A few days later, Ralph gave her a package with the admonition, "Don't open until Christmas." Christmas morning showed it to be a $150,000 ruby-and-diamond necklace with matching bracelets—from Cartier's, of course.

Meanwhile, Patricia divorced Wolfson and Ralph obtained a Mexican divorce. Ruth, ignoring the questionable Mexican divorce, filed her own divorce action in Chicago. Although at that point everyone appeared to be single, the planned wedding never quite came off. Sometime between Christmas and spring, while other things were blossoming, the romance withered.

The exact cause was never really clear; both claimed to the end that they had been jilted. Patricia said she was crushed and disillusioned, at least temporarily, by the discovery that Ralph had "deceived" her about his marital status at the time he had proposed marriage. She also charged he broke off the relationship when confronted with the perfidy. Stolkin insisted she used a "misunderstanding" about the Mexican divorce and his ex-wife's reluctance to sign a property settlement as an excuse to give him "the kindest and most gentle kiss-off" he'd ever seen.

Ralph then asked for the love gifts to be returned, but Patricia refused his request. Stolkin now felt he'd been duped, victimized, and taken. Ralph easily could have chalked his financial losses up to the price of experience, but he had no intention of accepting this kind of "kiss-off" from his former fiancèe, and even more strongly felt that when a woman breaks an engagement and refuses to marry a man, it does not grant her the right to keep an engagement ring, wedding gifts, as well as the residence intended as their marital abode. He filed suit to recover, not all of the gifts, but at least the return of the ring, the necklace, bracelet set, and the Knightsbridge flat.

Ralph didn't relish being in the public eye nor was he particularly enchanted with the apparent disdainful attitude of the British court. But he felt his cause was just and was determined to go through with the trial.

When it started, the trial seemed to be more of an international social function than a matter of determining justice. The press had a field day reporting every word of testimony and every move of the participants and their lawyers, both in the courtroom as well as out. Bejeweled and fur-muffled ultrafashionables from at least three continents flew in for the event in such numbers that one British journalist was led to remark there was so much mink and diamonds in evidence that the scene resembled the show counter at Tiffany's more than a courtroom. The holiday atmosphere did nothing to improve the disposition of Justice Melford Stevenson, a classical British jurist, who presided over the trial.

Justice Stevenson was clearly reluctant to try the case, and obviously didn't feel the Queen's Court should be compelled to listen to, let alone adjudicate, lover's quarrels among the idle rich. Shortly after the trial began, he was asked if a witness could be excused after concluding his testimony. The justice acceded with the remark, "I congratulate you on being able to leave this court." On another occasion, he removed his spectacles, banged them down on the bench, dropped his head into his hands, and was heard to mutter, "Why must I wade through the evidence of these miserable proceedings?" The "miserable proceedings" consisted of a plethora of witnesses parading in and out of the box in support of each side's numerous charges and countercharges.

But the crucial point in the trial came when Patricia's barristers sought to introduce tape recordings of transoceanic telephone conversations between Ralph and Patricia. The barristers admitted four separate taped conversations. Several were vital to authentication of her story about the breakup. However, after our electronics expert examined them, he indicated the tapes incomplete and possibly doctored, at which point we raised a vigorous attack on their admittance as evidence.

The tape dispute proved to be the breaking point for Justice Stevenson, whose distaste for the litigation was markedly increasing as conflicting testimony piled up. He began by castigating Patricia's legal counsel and ended once more with outspoken condemnation of the whole proceeding.

"The best service a lawyer can render to his client," he intoned in that dryly scornful manner for which British jurists are justly famous, "is an appearance, at any rate, of candor. It has not been very obvious so far."

As the lawyers squirmed uncomfortably in their wigs and robes, he went on to say, "It is clear to me that there has been deliberate deception in this court, particularly in the nondisclosure of tapes, and I say there is a heavy odor of suspicion over these matters."

Patricia's lawyers finally agreed to provide us with duplicates of the tapes, and Justice Stevenson said he hoped they could be compared with the transcripts and some agreement reached between us without him having to listen to them. He added, "I hope it can be done with goodwill and common sense, as nothing would make a more disastrous impression than people trying to be cunning, to keep something up their sleeve." He concluded, "If there is ever any sign of goodwill in this case, no one will be more pleased than I."

The "goodwill" didn't prevent the trial from dragging along for another two days. Finally, Justice Stevenson's general attitude and the conflicting and contradictory testimony of both clients convinced the lawyers it might be to everyone's advantage to negotiate a settlement, or at least give it another try. After court recessed, we went into a conference that lasted until after 3 A.M. With still no settlement acceptable to both sides, later that morning we went back to negotiating and reached an agreement in the corridor just before court convened, saving ourselves from another day of Justice Stevenson's increasingly acerbic commentary.

When the barristers announced to the court that a settlement had been reached and started to explain its terms, Justice Stevenson interrupted and said, "You need not tell me anything about the terms of settlement. It is perhaps fortunate for the parties and their advisors that I am relieved of making any comment." Under those circumstances we agreed not to reveal the terms of settlement, much to the displeasure of all the notables who had packed the courtroom throughout the trial.

Patricia and her mother left the courthouse by a circuitous route to avoid the waiting crowd and press, and Ralph went back to his hotel after expressing satisfaction with British justice in general. Patricia sent him an invitation to meet for a farewell drink, which was widely reported, along with the undenied speculation that the settlement involved the sale of the jewelry and the flat, the proceeds of which were to be divided evenly. The farewell drink rendezvous never materialized, however, and Stolkin returned to the United States.

The Stolkin affair left me with a strong sense of uneasiness, for something **is** seriously wrong when the legal or social formalities and trappings of marriage can so dominate relationships between people that it destroys them. It was plain that both Ralph and Patricia overemphasized the importance of getting married at the expense of what probably started out as a reasonably romantic situation, which might have turned into real love. If their effort had been placed on building the relationship instead of on the legal status of their prior marriages, most of their problems might have been avoided, or at least resolved, without the need for the public spectacle that ensued.

CHAPTER EIGHTEEN

What Is Marriage?

The requirement that a woman be licensed like a pet in order to be recognized as a wife and be accorded the law's protection seems both anachronistic and unfair. Yet Michelle Triola Marvin found herself in exactly this predicament when her mate, actor Lee Marvin, suddenly took off and married (licensed) his high school sweetheart.

Michelle was a talented young singer and actress whom I'd known early in my career as a tenant in one of my mother's apartment buildings, when she asked me to handle her divorce from actor Skip Ward. At the time Marvin first met her on the movie set of *Ship of Fools*, his fourteen-year marriage was on the rocks, and he was in the process of getting a divorce.

Michelle was the last person I would have expected to attract a hard drinking, free-living, and outspoken character like Marvin, since she had been raised in a strict Roman Catholic family. But within a few weeks of their first meeting, he had moved into Michelle's Hollywood Hills apartment, and for the next six years, including the night he won an Academy Award for *Cat Ballou*, Michelle was his almost constant companion. In some states, she could have claimed status as a common-law spouse, but California doesn't recognize common-law marriage, and a putative spousal relationship requires that at least one of the parties believes he or she is married. Michelle not only knew they weren't married, she didn't believe a license necessary for the relationship. From a moral standpoint she didn't think they could marry because her religion neither allowed divorce nor recognized civil divorce decrees.

Except for the license, however, she was Marvin's wife in every respect: she shared his bed, maintained his home, cooked his meals, and provided him with constant love and companionship. Socially, too, Lee and Michelle were accepted as a couple in Hollywood circles, though most of their friends doubtless knew they weren't actually married.

"We discussed marriage," Michelle told me, "but only in a negative way. We felt we didn't need a piece of paper to make our relationship real. We were together because we really wanted to be, although I would have done anything Lee wanted, including getting married, in spite of my religion's view on the matter."

Marvin's own feelings on marriage were a matter of public record. "It stinks!" he was quoted as stating outside the courtroom when his divorce was granted. Michelle accepted that view, as she accepted practically everything else he said or did, including his demand that she give up her career to be with him.

The career question cropped up early in their relationship when Marvin was in England filming *The Dirty Dozen.* Michelle had accepted a series of nightclub engagements in Hawaii, but cancelled the whole thing when Lee called her one morning and bluntly told her, "If you're not here in forty-eight hours, you can forget the whole thing." Michelle had no illusions about what was meant by "the whole thing" and took the next flight to London.

When the couple returned to California, they moved into a Malibu beachfront home, with what Michelle called "an understanding" that she would devote herself to home and Marvin completely. She also said it was "understood" her career was over, and whatever they earned while together would be shared.

For all intents and purposes, she became a Malibu housewife. Marvin's children by his first wife became frequent visitors, and neighbors and tradespeople called her "Mrs. Marvin." When he went away on film assignments or business trips, Michelle usually accompanied him, traveling as Mrs. Lee Marvin. In fact, one day in Baker, Oregon, where Marvin was filming *Paint Your Wagon,* a policeman who stopped her for a traffic violation recognized her and suggested, "You'd better have this driver's license corrected, Mrs. Marvin. In order to be legal, it has to be in your married name."

Their name differences became a problem with passport and customs officials, as well as with some hotel desk clerks. So when they returned from Oregon, Michelle asked my help to legally change her name "Triola" to "Marvin." Marvin knew what she was doing and apparently had no objections. I saw nothing unusual in the situation, since they had been together for so long by then that I considered her Marvin's *de facto* (by fact) wife, if not *de jure* (by law).

But it all ended with two phone calls one night in May of 1970. The first call came from a New York newspaper seeking her comments on Marvin's sudden marriage to his high school sweetheart. The second was from Marvin, confirming the marriage which she had initially considered some kind of "sick joke."

Later, Michelle told me they had quarreled before Marvin left on an East Coast publicity tour for his movie *Monte Walsh.* It was apparently not the kind of dispute that caused her any great concern nor was there any hint that it might lead to the end of their long relationship. Besides, she said, Marvin had called her regularly during the tour, even after he interrupted it to go to his dying father's bedside in Woodstock, New York. There was absolutely nothing in any of their conversations that prepared her for this stunning turn of events.

After the phone calls, she left the Malibu house in a state of confusion to stay with friends until she could handle the shock of the unexpected rejection. When she returned home, she found a note from Marvin's lawyer requesting a list of all the possessions she considered her own, so he would be aware of those items which would be taken when she left. "I had never thought about anything as belonging to Lee or to me," she told me later. "It was *our* home, and I considered everything in it as ours."

But when Michelle called the lawyers and told them as much, they informed her she had no legal claim to anything but her personal possessions and that Marvin wanted her out of his house before he returned with his new bride. Hurt and bewildered by the whole situation, Michelle complied with their demands and sought no legal counsel of her own. After Marvin came back to California, he met with her, promising to give her a modest monthly allowance for five years.

Michelle attempted to resume her career as an entertainer but found that five years out of the business is as good as being forgotten. She tried an office job next. That didn't work out either and she was let go. Then after a year Marvin cut off her allowance abruptly without notice or explanation.

When she finally came to me, Michelle was broke, frightened, and miserable, and asked but one question: Was there some way to make Marvin keep his promise about the four remaining years of monthly support payments? I told her that, considering the nature and length of their relationship, in my opinion she was entitled to a great deal more. I added that her status seemed no different from that of any other wife, even though she did not have a license from the state. Marvin had demanded, and she had given, everything that could be asked or expected of a wife. Under these circumstances I felt that she had a right to half of the assets acquired during the time they lived together as "man and wife." Anything less would not only be an injustice but, I strongly felt, probably unconstitutional as well.

The Fourteenth Amendment, which guarantees every citizen equal protection under the law, has been the keystone of most civil rights victories in this century. It has been utilized to ensure equity and block discrimination in almost every area of law and society except in the field of marriage or divorce, and toward people such as Michelle who are legally denied all rights to community property or spousal support solely because they are not state-licensed wives. In my mind, this kind of gross denial of equal protection raised an issue of "invidious discrimination" at least as serious as that described by the U.S. Supreme Court in the Meyes-Douglas case.

California seemed a good state from which to launch such a constitutional appeal. Common-law marriage is not recognized (which removes that question from consideration) and the state's community property laws, coupled with a liberal divorce law requiring an equal share division of assets, removes most other possible diversionary issues which would leave a clear-cut ruling on the basic constitutional question.

I explained my beliefs on the subject to Michelle, and she agreed it was very important that some precedents be set in this particular area of the law. She remained willing to test it even after I told her we'd probably lose in the lower courts, and any hope of a voluntary financial settlement might be ruined by the very act of raising the issue at all.

As my associate, Don Woldman, and I anticipated, the case was rejected first by the Los Angeles Superior Court in 1973, and later by the District Court of Appeal. The California Supreme Court, however, agreed to hear the case, which was argued before it in January of 1976 and is, at this writing, awaiting its decision.

There is a good possibility that Michelle's courage in standing up for her rights will result in new legal protection for the growing legion of noncertified wives who daily find themselves sharing her dilemma.

One of the principles most basic to meaningful discussion of modern marriage and divorce is recognition that the institution, with its medieval religious basis, is no longer totally relevant to the times. No matter what traditionalists say, the basic purpose and structure of family life and the family unit have undergone profound changes in the past hundred years and neither law, religion, nor social pressure can long maintain a system which has lost its practical value.

The latest Census Bureau statistics indicate marriage is declining for the first time since World War II, while the divorce rate has skyrocketed. Approximately half of the marriages now contracted end in divorce. Cohabitation outside legal marriage has increased by more than 800 percent since 1960. Many social, psychological, and scientific reasons are advanced to explain this unprecedented change in family life patterns, including the willingness of more people to abandon unsatisfactory marriages and the changing roles of women in educational attainment, employment opportunities, and economic independence. But I think one of the most significant reasons the concept of lifetime marriage is being abandoned lies in the fact that it is no longer economically necessary and, sometimes, not even socially desirable.

During the Middle Ages religious underpinnings were necessary to the institution of marriage to hold it together at a time when the world was still locked into an agrarian structure. In such a social order the individual family was the most efficient unit of production and the most practical factor for division of land or assigning of its stewardship.

But in an industrialized society, with economy based on technology and specialization of labor, the individual rather than the family has become the basic unit of production. The old roles and old rules, which rigidly defined the conduct and duties of each family member, have been significantly modified. Today the female members of our society have proven as capable of "manning" the machinery of commerce as men, and many women remain in the work force long after they get married, even when it requires a significant portion of their income to provide substitute household and child-care services.

If a marriage falls apart, there is often little real change in the woman's family role. Current census data show that more than 30 percent of our nation's minor children do not live with both natural parents. The family unit is further fragmented by the fact that children habitually leave home when they grow up and often find jobs in places or fields different than their parents. In addition, the state provides pension assistance for the aged, ending (or at least lessening) that area of family responsibility.

Under these circumstances, the traditional demand that one's marriage must last a lifetime, no matter how bad the bargain, is increasingly unworkable and unacceptable. Despite the significant legal bias against such unsanctioned relationships, countless couples today are forsaking formal vows in the same manner as Marvin and Michelle, which makes definitive judicial determination of their rights imperative to the ideal of equal justice before the law for all.

While the Fourteenth Amendment's equal protection clause is a basic issue, I think it will be necessary to redefine the meaning of marriage and reexamine the right of the state to regulate the institution before the issues can be fully resolved. A marriage is really nothing more than a partnership between two people who agree to share their lives. That makes it no more than a contract which should be subject to the same laws as any other contract. But, of course, it isn't treated like a regular contract because of the license requirement, which is the same as saying that a private business contract can't be enforced unless it has been recorded at the county courthouse.

Business contracts are, in fact, sometimes recorded as a matter of convenience, but the courts daily arbitrate and enforce thousands of unrecorded private contracts and oral agreements (Sam Goldwyn's reported opinion "that they ain't worth the paper they're written on" notwithstanding). It seems only fair that private marriage contracts (including unwritten agreements like those between Marvin and Michelle) should be afforded the same legal protection unless the state can prove there is still a valid and compelling reason to keep exclusive franchise power over the marriage institution. I don't think it can. The very same acts sanction the relationship in either case, except for the license and extralegal ceremony. But unless this compelling necessity can be clearly demonstrated, we cannot maintain two sets of values and still call ourselves a society pledged to equal treatment for all.

At best, state control of marriage can be justified as a convenience that provides a central registry showing who is married to whom. Such records are a valuable aid in determining bigamous relationships or paternity and, no doubt, significantly limit the scope and frequency of marital litigation. However, there is a serious question as to whether this convenience can justify the arbitrary exclusion of nonlicensed spouses from the legal system's protection. It has long been an unwritten rule of criminal law that it is better that a thousand guilty go free than one innocent man hang. Comparatively speaking, it would seem better that a thousand unnecessary civil lawsuits be filed than have one noncertified spouse be deprived of her or his rights for lack of a state license.

It isn't Michelle's purpose or mine to weaken or destroy the institution of marriage. Marriage and family life within the traditional boundaries of wedlock are a very satisfactory way of life for many people. But we are vitally interested in removing legal discrimination and, we hope, some of the stigma from unlicensed marriage relationships. In the long run, I think extending equal legal protection to unlicensed spouses may well *strengthen* the traditional system of marriage. After all, if a man knows he cannot escape the moral and legal responsibilities of a relationship, many of his reasons for avoiding formal marriage automatically dissolve and he is ready and willing to accept those commitments and duties and the responsibilities that go with them.

CHAPTER NINETEEN

Entering the Arena

Although experts in the domestic relations field differ on questions of cause and cure, almost everyone agrees that traditional marriage is in a state of crisis. I believe that it is the *doomability factor* in the marital mating process that contributes to its failure. People have always made mistakes, of course, so some failure factor has always been present, but the current "Do-your-own-thing-and-do-it-now" mentality has brought about a dramatic change in people's thinking. An increasing number of them no longer feel compelled to live with their mistakes. They find it simpler to change partners than to make the necessary changes to resolve relational differences. In our permissive society, I believe it is unrealistic to expect unqualified lifetime commitment to any institution, despite the verbal contract implications in the "till death do us part" marriage vows.

In addition to this current philosophy, there are a number of other reasons involved in creating the doomability factor. Among them is the fact that marital restrictions go against the nature of growth and change. Nobody is really the same person at forty he or she may have been at twenty. Time itself forces change, as does the matter of gender. A person's life is shaped by experience and environment, and in every social order, by virtue of being male or female, people necessarily encounter different experiences.

Even on isolated rural farms significant differences exist in the environments of field and house. The differences tend to increase sharply in urban environments where diverse ideas are widely communicated. It matters little whether a marriage follows the traditional breadwinner-homemaker pattern or whether both partners pursue separate careers; many couples still end up with each going his or her own way in divergent lifestyles until the doomability factor takes over, and they simply outgrow each other.

Before newer social attitudes and ethical standards took much of the shame and disgrace out of marital failure, marriages often "died" but they didn't end in divorce. People still went their separate ways, developed different interests, mistresses, or lovers, and sometimes watched their home life deteriorate into a series of angry confrontations and bitter fights. But the marriage remained intact, at least in name. The arrangement may have satisfied superficial requirements of church and state for preserving the family unit, but it usually played havoc with the mental health, happiness, and stability of the members involved.

Americans never really accepted the European idea of marriage, which was essentially a specialized business partnership. When we rejected kings, titles, and blood aristocracy, family-arranged "marriages of convenience" to enhance or consolidate social position became superfluous. Incurably romantic Americans wanted to marry for love; any other reason was degrading, disgraceful, and despicable. Remaining married once the honeymoon was really over could be justified by declaring it was a protection for the old folks and children within the family unit.

Now that the state has assumed "last-resort" economic responsibility for the social welfare of old people and children, plus full responsibility for education, family unit structure is of secondary importance. Marriage is a convenience, to be used and discarded when no longer functional. Remaining married after love has flown away is as undesirable as marriage without love. But while true love may well conquer all, the skyrocketing divorce rate indicates Americans are poorly trained in recognizing true love or in accepting the realities and conditions necessary to make marriage work.

Unfortunately, people seem even less prepared to deal with divorce than they are marriage. Very few—at least the first time around—have any idea of what to do once it is finally decided the marriage must be terminated. The spread of a do-it-yourself divorce movement in recent years has complicated the legal proceedings even more. The first question is no longer "How do I find a good lawyer?" but rather "Why do I need a lawyer at all?"

As to this last question, where there is a childless marriage and no real community assets, a person can sometimes handle his or her own divorce without legal and economic complications, providing the other spouse does not contest it. But the nominal fee most lawyers charge for their expertise in such actions is frequently worth the savings in time, effort, and eventual frustration. If children or property are involved, the old cliché, "A man representing himself before the court has a fool for a client," still applies. It's significant that even when the best divorce lawyers themselves are in the process of divorce, they appear in court duly represented by another colleague.

Selecting the "right" lawyer is sometimes the most difficult move in a divorce action, since many people (especially women) have little or no contact with attorneys on a professional level. Probably the most common way to retain one is through the recommendations of friends who know one through their own divorce or who are familiar with some lawyer's reputation in the field. Husbands and wives with careers usually retain a lawyer to handle their business affairs. One of the valuable services this person can render to a client would be to recommend a divorce specialist tailored to the party's particular need. Of course, since some lawyers and law firms do engage in general practice, they may agree to handle the divorce if it is relatively uncomplicated.

No matter how the initial contact is made, the most important decision in the selection is whether a client feels comfortable with the lawyer or not. Divorce is an intensely personal legal act. It doesn't matter how good the lawyer's reputation nor how great his legal expertise, if the client has little feeling of trust or confidence in him the results are likely to be unsatisfactory. Because this sense of rapport is so vital, a person should not hesitate to engage in "comparison shopping" if there are misgivings about the first lawyer contacted. But it should be understood one will probably be charged for the initial interview, even if the attorney isn't ultimately retained. A lawyer's time is money, and his services are usually billed on an hourly basis.

Since the client is paying for it anyway, there is little reason to be less than candid at the first meeting or hesitant about asking all the questions that come to mind, including the kinds of settlement possible and their cost. Bringing everything out in the open from the beginning provides an attorney with a good idea of what is involved and allows him to estimate fees in a more realistic manner.

Some clients are reluctant to discuss intimate details of marital misadventures with a comparative stranger, either from embarrassment or fear it might be used against them in court. They needn't be for two reasons: Anything told to a lawyer is kept confidential under the attorney-client privilege rule, and in order to plan the best strategy a lawyer must know as much as possible about the marriage and its problems. Marital misdeeds by either party can have a significant effect on settlement negotiations or child custody, even in states that have no-fault divorce laws.

In addition, if one is explicit and comprehensive in outlining problems and expectations during the initial interview, it helps establish ground rules for the legal relationship and reduces the number of common misconceptions clients tend to encounter.

One of the most common areas of attorney-client misunderstanding, especially among people who want "civilized" if not friendly divorces, springs from the adversary nature of the legal profession. Encouraged by what might be called "old ex-wives' tales" on how much easier a given divorce would have been if the lawyers hadn't made such a contest out of it, some people can't understand why both parties shouldn't use the same attorney. This position views a lawyer as some kind of referee who gives legal advice on the validity of the couple's arguments or decisions. That is the main function, not of the lawyer, but of the court, and the potential conflict of interest is so great few judges, if any, will try a divorce action when the same attorney represents both the husband and the wife.

Most judges realize that attorneys are only human and cannot represent two people without some bias or prejudice. There is also the very real likelihood that the judge's decision will be overturned later if an unhappy litigant claims he or she was not adequately represented by independent counsel. Divorce lawyers are expected to advocate the rights and interests of their clients as single-mindedly as business or criminal attorneys do their clients. Old ex-wives' tales notwithstanding, it is rare that two reputable attorneys will allow a personal legal contest to interfere with their client's best interests or for a trial judge to permit such activity to go unchecked.

Perhaps more disturbing to clients is the general atmosphere of cordiality and familiarity which characterizes relationships between lawyers. When opposing attorneys shake hands outside the court and begin inquiring about each other's wives and families, many clients feel they have become pawns in some kind of legal chess game and start worrying about the possibility of a "sellout." Such fears are almost always groundless and based on failure to recognize that the highly specialized nature of the legal profession creates natural social as well as business contacts among attorneys.

But it still nonetheless does not prevent two lawyers from becoming vociferous adversaries in court. After all, prize fighters can train at the same gym, party at the same nightclubs, and even live in the same neighborhoods without having it affect their determination to knock out their opponent once in the ring. College athletes have no problem in successfully competing with former teammates on opposing professional ball clubs. The law, too, is an adversary profession; lawyers are simply civilized combatants who fight, with words, in the arena of a courtroom.

Misunderstandings about lawyers' fees are another cause for needless client concern. This can easily be clarified by frank questioning during the initial interview. Unfortunately, many clients think lawyers should have a uniform scale and post a price list similar to the butcher's in a meat market. Others tend to assume the initial retainer fee covers the whole divorce action. However, getting out of a marriage is harder than getting into one—and much more costly. Immensely intricate questions involving community property, child custody, and spousal support make any attempt to set uniform standard divorce fees impractical, though most experienced lawyers have a good idea how much a divorce will cost once a client has outlined the major facts in the marital situation. Even so, any attempt to package and promote a fee schedule, similar to the butcher marking items in his meat case, would quickly bring an attorney before the disciplinary board of the bar association for unethical conduct.

How much lawyers and other professionals should charge for services has long been an issue of controversy. The old idea that a "workman should be worthy of his hire" is accepted by almost everyone—when applied to bricklayers and carpenters. Professional athletes or entertainers are seldom criticized for demanding as much as the traffic will bear in the sale of their talent. But if a doctor or lawyer seeks the full market price for his services, criticism is virtually universal.

Admittedly, it's hard to set a "fair market price" on life or freedom. A doctor is concerned with life, and a divorce lawyer is concerned with a person's freedom to enjoy that life under changing circumstances. As with all businessmen, the law of supply and demand dictates a lawyer's fees. But the divorce lawyer faces additional financial regulation from the court and, indirectly, his opposing counsel. Many states, including California, forbid lawyers to charge divorce clients on a contingency (or percentage of the judgment) basis, which is common in many other types of lawsuits. Thus, divorce lawyers charge for their services on an hourly basis (ranging from $35 to more than $100 an hour), according to the lawyer's skill, experience, and reputation. In addition, these may be extraordinary fees for extraordinary services and results.

In divorce actions involving significant amounts of money or property, the court is often asked to set and award attorney fees. This practice developed because the husband traditionally controlled the family finances prior to divorce, which could leave the woman without funds to pay for a lawyer. In California and other community property states, such court-awarded fees usually come out of community assets before division so it is in the best interest of the parties to remember that they are both paying for the attorneys. But it doesn't help a nervous client's state of mind when lawyers seem to argue more over their fees rather than the critical issues of the divorce.

The total costs of divorce can range from a few hundred dollars for a simple, uncontested case to sums in excess of a million dollars, but the attorney's fees are often a minor part of the total cost. Understandably, the more money and property a couple possesses, the more it will cost to divide equitably. There are accountants, tax experts, and appraisers who must be hired and paid to locate and analyze the couple's community assets. Sometimes it is necessary to hire private investigators to track down hidden assets. There are numerous deposition transcripts which must be purchased during pretrial discovery proceedings.

In today's complex economic situation, it is often advisable to employ the services of a financial consultant. In cases where assets are sizable and diversified, the services and advice of these financial experts can prove extremely valuable. One such expert, Ron Lerner, analyzed the financial position of a client whose husband's business interests were involved in a complex diversification and merger, and offered advice that ultimately helped enhance her financial position by several million dollars.

In many cases, knowing when and to what extent these experts should be employed is one of the elements that makes the use of a divorce specialist more advantageous, even if his charges seem higher than those of other lawyers in general practice. The lawyer needs to know early in the case to what extent he should employ such experts. This is another reason clients should disclose their full marital situation at the initial interview. Furthermore, the earlier an attorney knows about his client's marital circumstances, the quicker he can take the necessary action that will protect his client's interests.

It seldom makes any real difference who files for divorce first, since the court ultimately rectifies any inequities created by either party. But sometimes there is a psychological or strategic advantage to being first, especially for women. Husbands often attempt to conceal assets when it becomes obvious that a marriage is falling apart. Not infrequently, they attempt to hold their wives in line by threatening to toss them into the streets penniless if they don't behave. Such threats often make women fear to even think about getting a divorce.

Bank accounts and property can be placed under the control of the court at any stage of the divorce proceedings; of course, any temporary support is usually awarded long before the divorce trial is scheduled. However, there is often a psychological value in moving to restrain those kinds of husbands from selling property or draining bank accounts at the time the wife files the divorce papers. It lets him know that his wife has someone knowledgeable to look out for her, someone who will permit no nonsense, and it makes the wife feel more secure to know he can't leave her destitute.

Some clients, on the other hand, pose a different kind of problem for divorce attorneys. They are modern, civilized types who realize they can no longer live together but are determined to have a peaceable, friendly divorce. This is an admirable attitude but, unfortunately, too many forget that terminating a marriage is as much a business proposition as dissolving any other kind of partnership. Motivated by emotion or guilt, they tend to make agreements between themselves which they later regret, and which completely upset the delicate negotiations between the attorneys who are working to create a settlement that is equitable for both parties. Except where it concerns the most trifling items of personal property or furnishings, it is always best in all pre-trial negotiation to let the lawyers use the expertise and impersonal judgment for which they were hired. There is plenty of time for ex-husbands and wives to become friends after their marriage, which was made in heaven, has been settled in court.